At The Edge Of An Abyss

*A Story Of Holocaust Survival
Near The Death Camp Treblinka*

by

Michael Koenig

Mazo Publishers

At The Edge Of An Abyss

ISBN: 978-1-936778-74-4

Published by:
Mazo Publishers
P.O. Box 10474
Jacksonville, Florida 32247 USA
Tel: 1-815-301-3559

P.O. Box 36084
Jerusalem, 91360 Israel
Tel: +972-2-652-3877

Website: www.mazopublishers.com
Email: mazopublishers@gmail.com

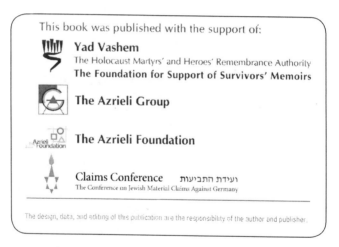

This book was published with the support of:

Yad Vashem
The Holocaust Martyrs' and Heroes' Remembrance Authority
The Foundation for Support of Survivors' Memoirs

The Azrieli Group

The Azrieli Foundation

Claims Conference ועידת התביעות
The Conference on Jewish Material Claims Against Germany

The design, data, and editing of this publication are the responsibility of the author and publisher.

Cover Concept and Design: Nomi Koenig
Cover Graphics: Frumi Chasidim

Note about the cover: The photograph of bones used on the front cover shows the remains of victims burned on the pyres in Treblinka.

The abyss…
where all reason and life
ceased to exist,

from which the tentacles
of a horrible demon
sucked in thousands
into its innards,

from which the stench
of burning bodies
permeated the air we breathed,

as we clung to the edge …
of Treblinka's abyss.

Contents

Acknowledgments   9
Foreword   10

Part One
At The Edge Of An Abyss

Life Before The War   16
  My Hometown   16
  Earliest Memories   17
  My Parents   30
  Anti-Semitism In Pruszków   34

War Breaks Out   35
  The Futile Odyssey   36
  The Siege Of Warsaw   38
  Return To Pruszków, 1939   39
  The Ghetto In Pruszków, 1940   42

The Warsaw Ghetto; 1941   44
  Life In The Warsaw Ghetto   46
  Escape From The Warsaw Ghetto   49

In Kosów Lacki   52
  The German-Russo War, 1941   55
  1942   56
  The Aktzyah In Kosów   62
  After The Aktzyah   65

Into Hiding   68

In The Barn – The Eleven Of Us 72
The Górals 75
The Barn 77
The Twelfth One 87
A Magic Moment Of Freedom 89
The Smell 90
The Ghoulish Act 92

Liberation 96

After Liberation 100
Return To Pruszków, 1945 103
The Paths Of Our Lives 104
Seeing Treblinka In 1944 106
Seeing Treblinka In 2000 108

Part Two
The Holocaust In My Poetry

The Abyss 128
O, Were All This But A Bad Dream! 129
The Barn 130
If Only You Could Have Promised! 131
The Fourth One 133
Zuch 134
The Rocks 135
The Hammer 136
The Fleeing German 137
It Could Have Been I...! 138
What Was He Thinking...? 139
O Tree In Treblinka! 140
It Is So Quiet In Treblinka Now! 141
How Can I Write...? 142
Where Was Humanity? 144
At The Museum Of Yad Vashem 145

Part Three

Speaking Out

The Poles And The Jews   148
Germans? Nazis?   151
One Cannot Comprehend!   154
Our "Free-Will" World   157
Crime And Punishment   160
Where Was He?   163
"They Should Have…"   166
Holocaust "Fatigue"?   170
Listen To Them Now!   172

Part Four

Assorted Thoughts And Memories

I Saw Hiroshima, 1945   176
On The USS General Sturgis –
From Europe With No Love   179
Just Waiting For The Question   182
Anne, I Understand…   185
How Could They Have Done It?   187
Idek And Marysia   189
Thanks, Dad!   193
The Hat   197
Oren Lubinski's Bar Mitzvah   199
This Has To Be Said   203
Some Thoughts   207

Photographs And Illustrations

Grandparents   17, 26
Father, Mother And Uncle Adam – ca. 1930   19
Before Darkness Fell   29
Mother – ca. 1939   31
Our Family Tree   32
Map Of Pruszków; (1930-1946)   40
Map Of Warsaw Ghetto   47
The Zylbermans' Family Tree   53
Map Of Central Poland
  (Pruszków, Kosów Lacki, Treblinka)   61
The Barn   81, 82, 83
Smoke Over Treblinka   91
Treblinka In 1944-45   107, 109, 111, 118
Railroad Tracks In Treblinka   113
Treblinka In 2000   116, 120, 121, 123
Register Of Jewish Survivors In Poland (Partial)   124, 125, 126
The Cattle Car   154
Before The Slaughter Began   158
Karl Hoeker, Kurt Franz   160, 161
Execution Of A Woman And Child   163
"Gott Mit Uns" Buckle   164
Remaining Section Of The Warsaw Ghetto Wall   177
The Warsaw Ghetto Area In 1945   178
All Set For A New Life   181
Letter To The Editor   206

The Enigma Of Man

He claims to be a creature
of compassion and justice...

So how does one explain
Treblinka and Auschwitz?

Acknowledgments

I wish to thank my wife Nomi, my brother Jerry and my sister-in-law, Linda for encouraging me to write this book. Were it not for their moral support, I doubt that I could have mustered the courage to bring up the memories of the painful past.

I owe my gratitude to my brother for the sketches he contributed and to his comments which helped refresh my memory.

My deep appreciation to Nomi for her helpful suggestions and the contribution she has made to the design of the front and back covers. For several years she has had to put up with countless hours of my sitting behind a closed door while writing this book.

I am deeply obliged to Linda for her devotion to this project as evidenced by her important contributions to the editing effort and the numerous suggestions she has made to promote this endeavor.

My thanks to Ms. Barbara Finch of Saint Louis, Missouri who so generously contributed her time to work on an early version of the manuscript.

My appreciation to my children Ami Lubinski and Steve Koenig and to my cousin Yakov Postolski for the assistance they gave me and the great interest they displayed in seeing this book published.

My deepest gratitude to Professor Yehuda Bauer of Yad Vashem for sharing with me his views on the subject of the Holocaust.

On September 1, 1939, a six-year-long eclipse of civilization plunged the world into darkness. Seventy-two years later, on September 1, 2011, I find myself putting the finishing touches on this work which describes my memories of those terrible years.

Michael (Mike) Koenig
Tel Aviv, Israel

Foreword

Between 1940 and 1945 six million Jews, one-third of the world's Jewish population, were murdered in an orgy of killing unprecedented in human history. This carnage, which history now calls The Holocaust, was planned and executed by the highest military and political echelons of Germany. The German military, their Slav collaborators and many local ethnic populations were effectively given a state license to murder Jews at will.

Through starvation, beatings, disease and deportations to ghettos and concentration camps, the victims were intentionally robbed of their dignity, dehumanized and, in the eyes of their persecutors, reduced to the level of pests to be exterminated.

Unimagined acts of brutality were employed to achieve this end. When murder by shooting or stuffing the victims into carbon monoxide-filled vans was deemed "inadequate", the process was changed until it became "efficient" enough to kill thousands every day in streamlined death-factory operations.

Among the six million victims were one-and-a-half million children. They were murdered in the most cruel and sadistic ways. Some were run over by tanks, some had their heads smashed against trees, some were tossed on top of the screaming victims in Treblinka's gas chambers; some were thrown into pits to be burned alive in Auschwitz.

Sixty-five years ago Germany decided that I, Michael Koenig, a Jewish child, had no right to live. But I was fortunate. I am a child survivor of the horrors of the Holocaust. At liberation my right to live was returned to me.

It is said that time heals and, to a certain extent, it does. It does so by blurring images and making bad memories less intense. Ironically, as years go by, this healing process, which has enabled so many Holocaust survivors to achieve normal lives, has become a source of concern to many of them. They are apt to question themselves: have they done enough to keep the memory of the Holocaust alive? Have they told as many people as possible the story of their survival? Have they written about it, recorded it, submitted it to museums for preservation in archives?

The voices of the victims were stilled forever with their last cries in the gas chambers. It did not require much imagination on my part to almost hear their voices as I walked the grounds of Treblinka a few years ago – parents frantically crying out the names of their children, the hysterical screams of "Mother! Father!", the death-throe screams of "Shema Yisrael"…

Certainly, there would also have been words which in the crush of death they had no chance to say:

"DO NOT FORGET US! DO NOT LET THE WORLD FORGET WHAT IS BEING DONE TO US!"

I began writing short pieces about my Holocaust experiences nearly 30 years ago. I have become keenly aware of the swift passage of time and have decided to commit my memories to print. I see this undertaking as fulfillment of my pledge to help preserve the memory of the six million of my people whose ashes lie scattered throughout Europe.

Of the Polish-Jewish population of 3.5 million in 1939, only some two percent, or 70,000, remained alive within Poland's pre-war borders. I consider myself very fortunate to be one of them. In addition, I belong to a family whose nucleus – my parents, brother and I – managed to remain together throughout the years of the Holocaust. It may be that there were other such lucky families, but it is my guess that their number was quite small. I have heard many Holocaust survivors tell their stories, each of them a unique, heart-rending tale of suffering and loss. What most of these stories have in common is that the survivors' families were almost always torn apart, with each family member left to fight for his life on his own. Children were separated from parents and siblings, husbands from their wives. Grandparents, uncles, cousins – all were forced to walk alone on their tortured paths to life or death. Families, entire communities, were rent asunder and ceased to exist. Occasionally, a survivor returned after the war from a concentration camp, a forest, or some other hiding place. Against this background, the story of my close family's survival intact is unique.

By now so many books on the Holocaust have been written that I cannot help but wonder what contribution my story can make. Nevertheless, I have decided to write because I feel it is my duty to do so. It is my part in not letting the world forget, my way to express the pain and outrage I feel about the indescribable crimes, which were committed against my people.

I did not keep a diary, and for some 30 years made no conscious attempt to recall or record what I saw and heard during the Holocaust. I began to record my memories in short pieces in 1979, after a high school girl here in Israel asked to interview me about my Holocaust experiences. Perhaps subconsciously, like so many others, I wanted to forget. I let the years slip by and the images of my youth retreat into the deep recesses of memory. But in reality, when some turn of events, or a question asked, prompts me to search my memory, the images return. Some are hazy and faded, others appear in sharp focus.

There is another, powerful, incentive for me to write. I was seven years old when the war broke out and thirteen when it ended. I now have grandchildren this age, and older. I feel it is my duty to tell them about our family's roots and describe the events which so dramatically affected our lives. I pray that they, and the generations to come, will learn from the past so they can wisely judge the intentions and actions of others. May they do all in their power to prevent terrible events, such as those which took place in my youth, from again plunging mankind into chaos.

I often wonder how our parents managed to cope with the terrible, psychological burden of the Holocaust. If I, then only a young boy, have been so deeply affected by it, then how much deeper must have been the scars our parents bore in their hearts till the end of their lives? I dedicate this book to their memory, and wish now to say in writing what I said to them while they were still alive: "Thank you, Mom and Dad, for having had the strength and determination to accomplish the nearly impossible – for saving our lives, and for managing to do it, against all odds, with all of us staying together." May you rest in eternal peace!

I dedicate these writings to the memory of the one-and-a-half million Jewish children who were murdered in the Holocaust (I could so easily have been one of them) and to the memory of "Feige's Baby", a newborn who had to die because she could not promise us not to cry.

In retrospect it is tempting to think of Holocaust survival as merely fate, at whose slightest whim life turned into death. It is true that countless events occur over which we have no control. However we also encounter many situations in which, by making certain decisions, we determine our own destiny. During the Holocaust such "fate-bending" decisions must have been made by my parents on an almost daily basis. But there were also two other families whose actions at certain critical points in time greatly affected our fate.

They were the Zylberman family, Jews who lived in the town of Kosów Lacki, and the Góral family, Polish Catholics who owned a small farm nearby. Had these two families not done what they did, and when they did it, we surely would have perished, either in the Warsaw Ghetto or in the gas chambers of Treblinka. To them we owe our eternal gratitude.

In addition, I wish to mention the Bienkowski family, Polish Christians from our hometown, Pruszków, who showed compassion by occasionally bringing us food when we were evicted from our home and forced into a ghetto. Their humanity is not forgotten.

Part One
At The Edge Of An Abyss

Life Before The War

My Hometown

I was born in 1932, the second son of a middle-class Jewish family. Our city, Pruszków, began to grow after the first world war. When I was born, its population numbered about 30,000. Approximately 3,000 of them were Jews. Pruszków possessed a solid industrial and commercial basis, which allowed its residents to enjoy a relatively high standard of living compared to other parts of Poland.

Though then considered a modern city, Pruszków, in the early 1930s, was, by today's standards, quite unsophisticated and rural. The streets were paved with cobblestones and became dirt roads a short distance from the city's center. Though connected to the national electric and water grids, its streets were lit with gas lamps and outdoor hand-operated water pumps were still in use. Outdoor toilets were common. Building height seldom exceeded two floors. Dank, dark courtyards were closed off from the streets by arched hallways and heavy wrought-iron gates, which were locked for the night. No automobiles were seen and telephones and radios were found only in the homes of the well-to-do. Linked in the 19th century to Warsaw by a steam railroad, and later by a modern, suburban, electric commuter train, the city developed into a major transportation hub between the capital and the western, industrial regions of Poland.

Today, the city is the home of Poland's largest rail works which provide employment for a large portion of its working class. Its proximity to the capital has been a powerful spur to its industrial development, and has greatly contributed to its growth. Many of its residents commute to Warsaw to work, and it draws much of its cultural sustenance from the capital's sophistication and worldliness.

Earliest Memories

In 1939, our household consisted of my paternal grandfather, Hanoch Kenigsztajn, my father, Isadore, my mother, Mary, and my brother Jerry (Jerzy in Polish) who is almost three years senior to me. We lived on the third floor of a four-story building at Kraszewskiego Street, number 12. My mother's side of the family consisted of her parents, Yakov and Henna Postolski, and her three brothers, Joseph (Joziek), Adam and Reuven (Rywek). They lived across the street from us.

I had the good fortune of having been born into an enlightened and loving family. My recollections of the years preceding the outbreak of the Second World War are of a normal, comfortable life. My paternal grandfather was a merchant who traded in commodities and held extensive property. Father assisted Grandfather in the daily running of the business.

In addition to the building in which we lived, we owned a modern slaughterhouse on the outskirts of town and a large farm estate called Albinów, located some 100 kilometers northeast of Warsaw. We spent many of our summer vacations there.

Paternal grandparents – Hanoch and Shaindla Kenigsztajn.

My earliest memories revolve around our home. Our apartment had a protruding balcony overlooking a cobblestone-paved street, and many of my first impressions of the world were glimpsed through the wrought-iron railings of that balcony.

What I saw was typical of a mid-sized Polish town of those days. The street was usually thronged with both gentiles and Jews. The Jews were easily distinguishable; many were smaller and darker than the ethnic Poles and some wore beards and black hats. Among the gentiles, the city folk were distinguished from the visiting villagers by their more sophisticated dress and manner. (There was a wide cultural and behavioral gulf between these two segments of the Polish population. The villagers were easily identified by their dress and they spoke Polish with a crude dialect, in contrast to the cultured version of the city dwellers.)

Below the balcony I remember seeing horse-drawn wagons rumble by on their iron-rimmed wheels. The wagons were usually loaded with sacks of country-grown produce. The peasants accompanying the wagons were dressed in baggy pants, rough cotton shirts and they wore high boots. The air was filled with their shouts of "Vyo!" to make the horses move and "Brrrr!" to make them stop. Sometimes they brought their families with them: women in wide, patterned skirts and colorful shawls on their heads and raggedly dressed, barefoot children. Frequently, in order to lighten the load, the peasants walked alongside their wagons. Occasionally a black cab, called "doroshka" would come into view, its driver snapping his whip at the horses.

For a boy barely out of his baby carriage, all I saw was new and fascinating but there were events which took place fairly regularly under our balcony and left on me a deeper impression than others. One of them was the Polish Independence Day parade. The Poles seem to love their drummers – the parade was inevitably led by a number of them beating out a cadence in perfect precision. Then came a sea of red-and-white flags topped with the crowned Polish eagle. The bands played lively marches and the soldiers proudly marched in step singing patriotic songs. Cavalry galloped by, the famous "Ułani" sitting erect on their shiny horses, the light from

(L-R) Father, Mother and her brother, Uncle Adam, ca. 1930.

their sabers reflecting into my eyes. Scouts and school children followed and it would take some time before the excitement of the parade would subside.

Another event, a more frequent one, was the Polish funeral. Poland was, and still is, a deeply religious, Roman-Catholic country. Apparently, the funeral processions were meant not only to bring the deceased to their burial places but also to involve the local population and re-affirm their religious beliefs. There was a church near us and the funerals always passed our home. The singing and the tinkling of bells would alert me to their coming. The bells were swung by young boys clad in white robes. At the head of the procession a huge cross was carried, followed by a priest intoning prayers.

As the procession approached, the pedestrians on the sidewalks crossed themselves and knelt with their heads bowed. I felt uneasy watching them. I knew this was "their" religion and that we didn't kneel on sidewalks and didn't kiss the hands of passing priests. I felt fear... the black-robed priests were to be avoided. I recall ducking into gates of buildings whenever encounters with them seemed likely.

We had a three-room apartment. On the right side of the entry hall was a bathroom and adjacent to it a room with a bathtub. On the left side was the entrance to the kitchen and at its end a door leading into the first room. The bathroom brings back memories of my screaming in terror when, judged to be too old to sit on the potty, I was first put on the seat. The bathtub evokes memories of my brother and me playing with plastic ducks and begging Mother for a bit more time to splash in the pleasant warm water. I remember yelling when my hair was being washed and soap suds got into my eyes.

The kitchen fascinated me the most. It was always warm and cozy, and I spent a lot of time there watching mother and the maid going through all the activities associated with running the household. There was much cooking and baking going on there on the coal-fed stove. I remember watching the maid scrubbing the blackened pots and pans after every meal. Dough was kneaded, flattened and rolled on a wooden board. Mother's fingers moved with amazing speed as she cut it into thin noodles or formed it into thumb-sized dumplings called "kopytki". The delicious aroma of baking cookies often filled the house; my favorite ones were called "herbatniki". They tasted great with tea.

The kitchen also served as the laundry room. Bi-weekly laundry days were laborious, elaborate productions. The laundry was boiled on the stove in large pots. A huge, round, wooden tub, called "balia", was brought into the kitchen and filled with numerous buckets of boiling water, to which a blue liquid was added. Through clouds of steam I watched the maid vigorously rub the dirty laundry against a metal washboard. A wringer was mounted at the edge of the tub and the washed clothes were fed through hand-cranked rollers. I loved to watch the water spill back into the tub with every turn of the handle. The clean clothes were placed in baskets and taken up to the building's attic to be hung out to dry.

When I was old enough, I was allowed to go up to the attic. The place was semi-dark and mysterious with the smell of wet laundry filling the air. Clothes were hung from ropes tied to thick wooden beams which slanted up toward the peaked roof. At the end of the attic there was a small, round opening which allowed some light and air into the room. I would slowly inch my way up to it and carefully look outside. Our building was one of the tallest in town, and the height made my dizzy. Although I knew that I was safe, my heart beat with fear and excitement. Down below I could see a coal-and-lumber yard. To the left I saw the walls and the chimney of a porcelain factory. Straight ahead was a short street called Krótka, with a row of low buildings housing small shops. One of them particularly sticks in my mind: a store where we used to buy delicious salted herring and pickles out of a barrel.

The rooms in our apartment were serially connected; we had to pass through the first to get to the second and through the second to get to the third. The first room was small, and contained a desk with a black telephone on it and a beautiful, glass-fronted set of bookshelves. There was a blue-and-white Jewish National Fund collection box on the wall, along with a painting of the Western Wall in Jerusalem.

The second room contained a large dining table flanked by high-backed chairs. This was where we ate our meals. To the right stood a bookcase, and on the left a tall, dark grandfather's clock.

Its ticking, swinging pendulum and hourly chimes fascinated me; I learned to tell time from its grey face. In the far corner stood a black grand piano with gold letters spelling "Bechstein" on the front panel.

The third room served as the family's bedroom. It was heated by a round, upright coal-fed stove with a pipe leading up to the ceiling. I heard it said that in this room Grandmother Shaindla passed away, just a few days before my birth. (The story was that like a good, Jewish housewife, her last words were questioning whether the laundry has been hung up in the attic.)

My crib, and later my bed, were in this third room. Strangely, the image which persists in my mind is that of a triangle of light on the ceiling of this room. The light formed in the evening whenever the door between the second and third room was left ajar. I was put to bed early while the grownups continued to sit and talk in the adjoining room until late in the evening. I would stare at this patch of light with childish fantasies swirling through my mind until sleep closed my eyes.

A little violin rested on top of a black clothes closet. I always looked at it before falling asleep. I don't know how old I was when it first appeared there, but I remember being told that when I reach my seventh birthday, I'll start taking violin lessons. There was a reason parents made this decision. As an infant, I would sit wide-eyed and listen to mother play the piano and sing. She had a lovely voice and I used to join her in duets at every opportunity, both as a child and as a grownup. When the wing of the piano was open, I would stand on my tip-toes and stare in wonder at the felt-covered hammers striking the chords. Somehow, out of all this seemingly chaotic, random motion, a sweet Chopin melody would emerge.

Sometimes Mother's teenage cousin, Moniek, would visit us and play his violin to Mother's accompaniment. Those tender sweet tunes tugged at my heart. My obvious fascination with the violin must not have escaped my parents' attention, for one day that small slender-necked violin appeared on top of the clothes closet.

But my musical education was not to be. Four months after my birth, Adolph Hitler came to power in Germany. The world was fast approaching the most cataclysmic period in its history. Six weeks before my seventh birthday, Hitler's hordes invaded Poland. For the next five years our thoughts were focused solely on survival.

Polish winters are severe, and the water pipes in our apartment would often freeze. I looked forward to this happening because then a man named Wiewior would come to visit. A heavy-set man, Wiewior always wore a leather jacket. He would puff his way up the stairs to our apartment, set his tool-box on the floor, and joke with us children. When he opened the box I would stare in amazement at his various strange-looking tools. The aroma of metal and oil filled the room. The tool I most loved to watch him use was his acetylene torch. He would turn its knob and touch the hissing spout with a burning match. As if by magic a strong, roaring, pink-blue flame would shoot out. Then he would climb a ladder in our bathroom and, using the torch, thaw out the pipes.

I used to love to watch Father shave in the mornings. He shaved in our third room, which gave me the opportunity to watch him from my bed. Unlike many Jews of that period who wore beards, Father and Grandfather Hanoch were clean-shaven. First, Father prepared a white lather in a bowl; then he applied it to his face with long, swinging strokes. Using a small short brush he would work it into his whiskers with circular motions. This lathering took a long time. Then he would sharpen a long razor blade (I can still hear the whipping sound as he repeatedly slapped it against a leather belt.) Finally, he would press the razor blade against his face and begin to remove the lather with long, smooth strokes. Fascinated, I watched as his face slowly emerged from underneath the snow-white layers. I cringed whenever he cut himself (I didn't like the sign of blood), but he would rub the cuts with some stick and, as if by magic, the bleeding would stop.

I was not a good eater in my early childhood. I passionately disliked the cooked sweet vegetables so characteristic of the Polish-Jewish diet. My two most-hated vegetables were spinach and the cooked sweet carrots called "tzimes" in Yiddish. Close behind were boiled chicken and its derivative, the chicken broth called "yoych". Large eyes of chicken fat floated on the surface of this hot soup, while thin noodles insidiously hid at the bottom of the bowl. I dreaded the traditional Friday evening dinners which were replete with such "delicacies". Grandfather often brought home from the synagogue some poor person to eat with us on Shabbat.

The only foods I really enjoyed were the traditional sweet braided bread called "challah" and the delicious home-made "gefilte fish". I remember Mother saying to us boys: "Eat, children, eat! If war comes, there will not be enough food." Apparently by then clouds of war were thick enough to be brought to the attention of even a small Jewish boy in Poland. Unfortunately, Mother had no idea how prophetic her words were.

My brother, Jerry, under Father's guidance, became an ardent stamp collector. I remember the evenings devoted to sorting the stamps and gluing them into albums. Because we used the white of raw eggs for glue, we could work on the albums only when a cake was to be baked. I was deemed too young to touch the stamps, because I might damage their edges. Jerry used to lay the stamps out on the table, and I was not allowed to breathe hard near them. Nevertheless, I tried to make myself useful. I would run into the kitchen and emerge triumphantly holding the empty shells of freshly broken eggs. I balanced them carefully so the precious white sticky liquid would not spill. Jerry's collection included stamps from all over the world. The ones which made a lasting impression on me were those from Palestine, which showed the Tower of David, the Western Wall, and Rachel's Tomb. (When I first visited these sites some 30 years later, I experienced a curious flashback to those stamp-gluing evenings at home in Poland.) The stamp collection must have been quite valuable, since it and Father's camera were the only two things missing when we returned home after being forced to leave it for a short time at the outbreak of the war.

The ground floor of our building housed a greengrocer's shop and a butcher. We shopped on a daily basis. The produce and dairy products were plentiful, wholesome and tasty. There was no refrigeration. We stored perishables in the cool darkness of the building's basement, where every tenant had his own compartment. There, small heart-shaped sacks of milk dripped slowly, drying into a delicious cottage cheese. Jars of milk were also stored there. When fermented, this "sour milk" tasted wonderful on hot summer days, especially when spread on mashed potatoes.

Cabbage was another menu staple. A bowl half-filled with mashed potatoes and half by steaming sour cabbage was my favorite. Fresh baked goods and various sausages were delicious. Milk was bought fresh daily, but both milk and water had to be boiled before drinking. I remember how surprised I was when I first saw Americans drinking water straight from the faucet.

Also, near our apartment were a bottling shop and a bakery. At times Grandfather would take me to the bottling plant to exchange empty bottles for full ones. I liked the soda water for its bubbles and the tickling sensation they produced. From the bakery came the large disks of matzo baked for Passover. On Fridays I watched from the balcony as women carried huge metal pots of chulent (the traditional Jewish stew of meat, potatoes, beans and barley) to the bakery to be baked overnight for the Sabbath.

Once a week an open-air market, called a "targ" was held in town. I enjoyed going there with Mother and the maid. The day before the market, rows of horse-drawn wagons would roll into town. Farmers brought their produce, vegetables and colorful shawls and trinkets to a large, empty lot, where they displayed them spread out on the ground or in booths. The air was filled with the cackling of chickens, the smell of manure and the cries of the peddlers.

My maternal grandparents lived across the street from us, on the first floor of a two-story building. I remember little about them, except that Grandmother Henna had her hair pulled back in a bun and had a wart on her face. Grandfather Yakub, a tall, bald man with a small mustache, was a flour merchant. They were deported with us to the Warsaw Ghetto and from there were, most

Maternal grandparents – Henna and Yakub Postolski.

likely, sent to their deaths in Treblinka. We have a postcard they sent us from the ghetto – a sad reminder of grandparents whom I hardly knew.

Pruszków is connected to Warsaw by a modern electric train (then called EKD) and also by a conventional, then steam-driven, railroad. I remember the EKD for its smooth, quiet rides but, also, for the "Juden Verboten" (Jews Forbidden) signs prominently displayed on its wagons during the German occupation. I remember the steam-driven train for a different reason: what a thrill it was to stand with my kindergarten class under an overpass and wait for the train to pass overhead! It was dark in the tunnel with rays of sunshine filtering in from the sides. First came the whistle, and then from a distance we heard the approaching thunder of wheels. Closer and closer they came until, with an earsplitting roar, they rolled overhead. We giggled and shouted for joy trying to make ourselves heard over the din. After that we often had a picnic on the banks of a small nearby stream. We picked flowers, made wreaths, and listened, wide-eyed, to the fairy tales which our teacher, Lonia, told us. Sometimes we walked in the nearby park, paired off and holding hands for safety. We strolled in the shade of oak trees and delighted in gathering shiny, brown chestnuts. I often walked with my cousin, Gutek, a quiet boy with large brown eyes. He always wore a beret as many little boys did in those days. I lost track of him in the Warsaw Ghetto. He did not survive – murdered, most likely, in one of Treblinka's gas chambers.

The memory of the EKD train is of walks with my family along its tracks to a pine forest in nearby Komorów. I loved to run among the trees and pick mushrooms. We usually had a picnic lunch, I played with Jerry and wrestled with Father. There was no swimming pool in Pruszków; in order to swim one had to go to a remote place called Glinki, a dangerous clay pit where drownings were frequent. I recall the delight of occasionally going to the Maccabi swimming pool in Warsaw and joyfully frolicking with Father in the water. Since I was just seven years old when the war broke out, I missed out on all the activities children my age normally engage in, such as school, sports and games. I learned to ride a bike and swim only in my teens, after the war.

Our photo album contained a picture of me when I was only eight days old – a plump ball of flesh, round-faced with intensely staring eyes. In fact, I used to stare at light so intensely, without blinking, that my parents feared I might have been born blind. I remember looking at that photo and wondering whether this naked baby, lying on his tummy was really me. Mother wanted to have a girl, having already been blessed with the birth of a boy. For some time she did not cut my hair and tied it with ribbons. But eventually I began to pull off the ribbons and my hair was cut, thus affirming my masculinity. I was probably about three years old, when, on one of our vacations in Albinów, I bit a dog on his ear. I heard laughter around me and someone called me "Hitler". I had no idea what this word meant but, apparently, by that time Hitler had already managed to make a bad name for himself.

Our home was traditional. Grandfather prayed daily. I watched him sway and murmur, his forehead adorned with a black case, his arm tied with a black leather strip. At times he took me with him to the synagogue. I have dim memories of walking through a narrow passage between homes and emerging into a courtyard, in the middle of which stood the synagogue, a low, wooden structure. I did not feel comfortable in the crowd of the worshipers. Maybe, given more exposure to the religious aspects of Judaism, I might have overcome this feeling of discomfort. I did enjoy waving small flags and turning noisemakers on the holiday of Purim and watching the candles and listening to songs on Hannukah. The dietary laws of "kashrut" were observed in our home, with separate dishes for dairy and meat. On Friday before sunset, Mother, her head covered with a kerchief, lit the Sabbath candles and recited the blessings.

The only Jewish school in town was housed in the upper floor of our building. Jerry attended this school for a while. Prodded by the rabbi, he came home one day and asked to wear a small prayer shawl, known as the "tales kutn", under his shirt. He cried when Father denied his request. This incident marked the end of Jerry's religious education. My education, of any kind, was not to begin until after the end of the war.

My parents were strong Zionists. Already at an early age I realized that the blue-and-white Jewish National Fund collection box on the wall signified a deep, emotional connection between us and a far-off land called Palestine. There existed a number of Zionist activity groups in town. In the 1920s several Jewish families left Pruszków to settle permanently in Palestine. Uncle Rywek spent some time there paving roads around the settlement of Rishon LeTziyon.

We spoke the Polish language correctly in our home. This may seem like a strange statement – surely citizens of a given country should be able to properly use the country's language. But this was not true for large portions of the Polish-Jewish population. The Jewish people, particularly in rural areas, tended to live in closed communities, called "shtetls", where they were able to conduct their daily activities using only Yiddish. The need to speak Polish was limited to encounters with gentiles, mostly in business transactions. The result was Polish spoken with a heavy, easily identified Yiddish accent. During the Holocaust this proved to be the undoing of many a Jew who tried to pass himself off as an ethnic Pole (undoubtedly, the other two major factors, which made survival difficult, were the Semitic features of many Jews,

Before Darkness Fell – Vacation in Kazimierz, 1938

Mother with her brother Rywek.

(L-R) Jerry, Father and I.

I'm in the driver's seat; Jerry is behind me.

At the EKD train station in Pruszków. (L-R) I, Mother and Jerry.

and the fact that the Jewish males were circumcised whereas non-Jewish males were not).

The times I heard Yiddish spoken at home were when we had some Yiddish-speaking person visiting us. I was not to be fully exposed to this unique, versatile language until the Holocaust years. Then I was surrounded by people who used it as their everyday means of communication.

At times our parents would take us for a day in Warsaw. It was exciting to walk through the busy, gaily-lit streets of the big city while tightly holding on to a parent's hand. I loved the electric streetcars, with their bells and clangs, and stared in amazement at these modern-day wonders.

In the summers we often vacationed at our farm, Albinów, near Kosów Lacki (pronounced 'Kosoov Lahtzkee'), a small town about 100 kilometers northeast of Warsaw. A tree-lined path led from the road to the main compound of the farm. On both sides of the path, as far as the eye could see, lay fields of wheat and rye, with patches of sunflowers interspersed among them. The thick sunflower stalks bent under the weight of the huge, gold-rimmed heads, chocked full of delicious black seeds. As we spent our careless summer vacations there, little did we realize that, just a few years later, Kosów Lacki and its surroundings would play such a crucial role in our struggle for survival.

In 1938 we took a trip to the resort town of Kazimierz on the banks of the Vistula River. This fragrant, mountainous countryside was enchanting. Holding hand-carved canes purchased from a local souvenir shop, we climbed hills to explore the ruins of old castles. We returned to Warsaw on a steamer along the Vistula River.

My Parents

Photographs of Mother in her youth attest to her delicate beauty. Her finely-shaped face and beautifully-framed eyes rendered her quite attractive. Her hair was usually pinned back in a bun, or sometimes she wrapped her long braids in a crown-like fashion around her head. I remember her saying, lightheartedly, that she got compliments on having "the nicest legs in town". She retained much of her beauty until the end of her life.

Father, who was nine years older than Mother, began to court her when she was only 15. He used to wait for her at the gate of her high school and carry her books. Mother was embarrassed to admit that he was her suitor and introduced him as her brother. Though she exasperated him on many occasions, he remained in love with her for the rest of his life, through more than 50 years of

Mother, ca. 1939.

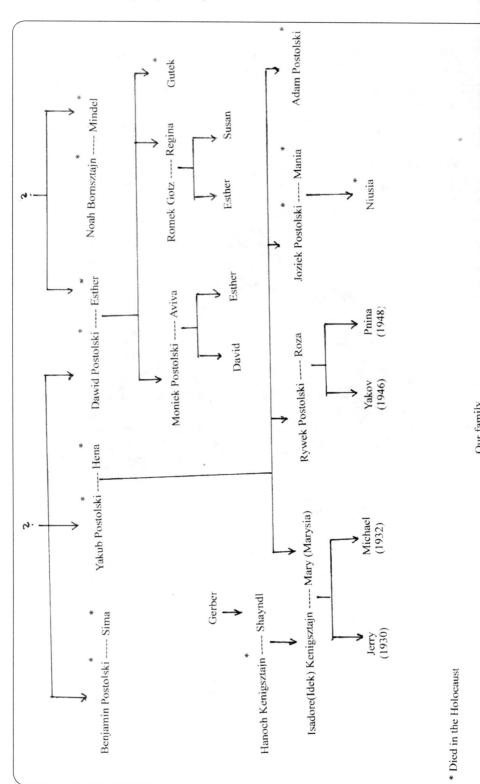

Our family

* Died in the Holocaust

marriage. When he was 76, he came alone to Israel for our son's Bar Mitzvah. He missed her so much that he vowed to never again go anywhere without her. And he did not. He passed away two years later, without ever being away from her again.

Father was a short, broad-shouldered man. In his youth he excelled in sports, such as soccer, swimming and light athletics. He had a round, fleshy face with slightly protruding ears. There was a certain sense of refinement and gentility about him. Despite being short, he was quite attractive to the opposite sex. His photographs show him as a finely-dressed, handsome young man. He was energetic and rather adventurous. He was always ready to try something new, much to Mother's frequent annoyance. He read a lot, was progressive in outlook, and placed great emphasis on education. He realized his dream of having both his sons become engineers – a dream he nourished in the days when even a high school education was a rarity.

Father whistled beautifully, and used his personal charm and infectious grin to impress people. He could move people to tears or laughter just by saying the right words at the right time. His bubbling nature sometimes gave rise to awkward situations, but he refused to allow any criticism to dampen his spirits.

Father was a loving, good-natured person. He frequently gave Mother a kiss and thanked her at the end of each meal. However, he could also be nervous and explosive. When he was excessively annoyed, his first response was to keep silent. Then his face would harden and his eyes would glaze over. We knew that an explosion was imminent. I feared those moments, but I also knew that his anger would quickly subside and that he would then return to his calm, loving self. He was a born optimist, and it was his optimism that saved us in the Holocaust.

As much as Father was an optimist, Mother was his opposite. (Years after the war, Mother told us that in the darkest days of the Holocaust, when things seemed hopeless, she suggested to Father that we all commit suicide. He categorically rejected this idea.)

Mother loved her home and her classical music and, above all, she wanted to have a quiet life. Sometimes when Father dreamed and planned, Mother would question and frequently throw cold water on his schemes. No doubt, many times he needed a dose of reality. His adventurous nature made him take many uncalled-for chances. But despite their differences, Mother and Father remained deeply in love until the end of their lives.

Anti-Semitism In Pruszków

In contrast to the love and security which surrounded me at home, I felt threatened and unwanted when walking the streets of my hometown. I was aware of the frequent attacks on Jews by Polish anti-Semites. The anti-Semitism in Pruszków was so ubiquitous and virulent that a Jewish child would begin to feel its humiliating effect from the first day he set foot outside his home. Jewish youngsters were frequently chased and jeered by Polish youth under the condoning eyes of their elders. Young children would follow us on the street chanting, "Jews to Palestine!" or "Jews killed Christ!". Some places, like the local park, were notoriously dangerous. No Jew would dare walk alone there. On one corner of town stood a statue of Holy Mary. Walking by it, often meant being chased and roughed up by hooligans, who lay there in wait for Jews to pass by.

I have very few good memories of the way the ethnic Poles behaved in those years toward their Jewish fellow-citizens. However, there were exceptions, and one was the Bienkowski family. Mr. Bienkowski was a tall, lean-faced man with thin-rimmed glasses. He was employed by our family in some administrative capacity. I heard that he ate six eggs for breakfast, and this made him, in my eyes, somewhat of a superman. Of the rest of the family I recall only their son, Jedrek, who was my brother Jerry's age and became his close friend. They took walks and played together, although in those days it was very uncommon to see Polish and Jewish children socialize. Ironically, Jedrek looked "more Jewish" than we did, and this sometimes led to his being chased by Polish hooligans while we were left alone.

War Breaks Out

World War Two broke out a month-and-a-half before my seventh birthday. We sensed the tension growing for weeks before the outbreak of hostilities. I heard the grownups speak in worried tones about the ominous events taking place in the world. The name Hitler became common in conversations and began to penetrate my consciousness. Many jokes were being told about Hitler, such as that he was nothing but a "frustrated painter", and the "Heil Hitler" raised-arm salute stemmed from his holding a brush while painting walls. But under this outward lightheartedness I could sense an ever-deepening layer of concern. Young men were being drafted into the army. Outside our windows, patriotic parades were being held. The Polish people were being rallied against the German threat, and the slogan most often heard vowed "not to yield to Hitler one inch of Polish territory and not one button off a Polish uniform."

On September 1, 1939, World War Two began with the German invasion of Poland. The windows of our apartment were reinforced with brown tape and covered with black cloth. Fearing a German gas attack, people walked the streets carrying improvised white-gauze masks to cover their mouths and noses.

The first overflight of German airplanes on their way to bomb Warsaw was greeted with jubilant cries of "Nashe! Nashe!" ("Ours! Ours!") by the people on the street, in the false belief that they belonged to the Polish (but largely non-existent) air force. During one such incident I recall hearing a faint rattle in the sky. I looked up and saw a small Polish aircraft firing its guns at the German armada. Moments later I saw the plane plunge in smoke toward the ground. Subsequent German overflights, along with the news that Warsaw was being bombed, created panic among us. When the air-raid sirens went off, some people were seen running into their homes while others were running out of them. I remember one incident; upon hearing the sirens, we ran out the door to seek shelter in the building's basement. What met our eyes was a scene of bedlam. Panic-stricken, crying people were running up and down the stairs. Those running up the stairs were doing so in order to be as high as possible in case of a gas attack. Those running down, were running for the basement to be as low as possible in case of a conventional bomb attack. In the end, the Germans, for reasons of their own, did not bomb Pruszków at all, and the town escaped any damage to its infrastructure.

The Futile Odyssey

The news of the Germans' rapid advance into Poland caused a major panic in Pruszków. Thousands left their homes in hopes of fleeing from the approaching danger. I remember the feverish preparations in our home as we were packing our belongings. Our already-taut nerves were further strained by our Polish maid Maria, who taking advantage of the chaos, absconded with some of our money. We loaded our belongings onto two horse-drawn platforms and left Pruszków. In no time at all, we found ourselves caught up in a surge of frightened humanity. The roads were crowded with fleeing people – some on foot, some on horses and others in horse-drawn wagons. It was becoming progressively more difficult to navigate our platforms through the increasingly dense throng. Polish army convoys were competing for road space with the fleeing refugees. A few kilometers out of town we were stopped at a roadblock. One of our platforms was unceremoniously dumped onto the road to serve as a barricade against German tanks. With a lighter load, but with heavier hearts, we proceeded on our way.

To this day I don't know in which direction we were heading – presumably eastward, since the Germans were advancing from the west. Did we have a certain destination in mind or was this a case of having been swept up in the general hysteria? I suspect the latter was true. Whatever the reason, the following days turned into an exhausting, dangerous odyssey.

We tried in vain to outrun the Germans. They always seemed to be one step ahead of us. Wherever we arrived, we heard the muffled roar of artillery and far-off bomb explosions. The horizon, often covered with black smoke, glowed an ominous red at night. Corpses of dead horses lay at the roadside. Exhausted families squatted along the way. We heard rumors that the Polish government had escaped to Romania.

It was open hunting season for the German air force. The German bombers enjoyed completely free skies, with no sign of Polish airplanes to oppose them. One day we came under air attack near a marshy forest. With a hellish scream, the airplanes dived one after another, their rattling guns strafing the forest and the surrounding area. Some Polish soldiers fired their rifles at them. I recall the deafening sound of a machine gun firing near us. Bullets began hitting the trees. Father threw himself over me to cover me with his body. He kept whispering encouraging words into my ear. Bullets ripped the bark off the tree under which we were lying. When the strafing began, just before we dove under the tree, I saw a bomb explode in the nearby patch of swamp, raising a cloud of black mud into the sky.

When the attack ended, while we were still getting off the ground, shaken by what had just occurred, we heard sounds of a commotion near us. To our disbelief, we saw a group of people surrounding Uncle Joziek, Mother's brother. They had his arms pinned behind his back and were dragging him away. We ran after them and were flabbergasted to hear that he is being accused of being a German spy! Someone claimed to have seen him using a mirror to flash signals to the German airplanes. He was taken to a group of Polish soldiers who wanted to execute him on the spot. We pleaded with them. Fortunately they relented and Uncle Joziek was released.

The Siege Of Warsaw

Many of the fleeing refugees (we were among them) eventually came to the conclusion that their attempts to outrun the Germans were futile. In their minds there was only one place which still offered some hope, and that was Poland's capital, Warsaw. I suspect that in the minds of many, the war was already considered lost, but apparently they still maintained the illusion that the tide might turn. After all, didn't England and France promise to come to Poland's rescue? And were they not assured by their government that the Polish armed forces would not allow "one inch of Polish soil" to fall into Hitler's hands? They had reason to believe that Warsaw would be heavily defended and, indeed, it was. I was too young then to appreciate it, but from what I have read in subsequent years, I learned that the Polish army put up a gallant fight against the German invader. But the Polish cavalry was no match for German tanks, and its outdated air force no competition for the German Luftwaffe. Of the four weeks it took the Germans to conquer all of Poland, two weeks were needed for them to crack the resistance of Warsaw.

And so we, together with tens of thousands of other desperate refugees, headed for the illusory safety of the capital. The Germans were right on our heels. Soon after we arrived they surrounded the city.

We found lodging with the Gerber family who were somehow related to my maternal grandmother, Shaindla. The Gerbers owned a small cheese factory in the backyard of their home. One member of the family worked in a bank.

The German siege of Warsaw immediately began to affect our lives. Food was rationed but it was the incessant, nerve-wracking artillery fire and bombing which affected us most. At times, while looking out of a window, I would spot a German fighter plane diving out of the sky with its characteristic whine, its machine guns firing. Sometimes squadrons of heavy German bombers would fly over and carpet-bomb the city. When the air-raid sirens sounded, we sought shelter in the basement. I recall huddling in fear with my family as the sound of explosions drew ever closer. I remember clinging to Father and asking him whether a bomb would hit us. In a quiet voice he would confidently assure me that it would not, and he always turned out to be right. We sighed with relief when the sounds of explosions began to fade away.

We were, understandably, distraught when one day the Polish army set up an anti-aircraft gun in the Gerbers' yard. When the gun fired, the noise was unbearable. We feared that its presence would make us a prime target for the attacking aircraft. Indeed, this is what happened. It was daylight when a German airplane decided to take care of this annoying gun, and dropped a bomb aimed at it. We heard the ominous sound of the approaching bomb and braced for the explosion, but it never came. When the all-clear sounded, we cautiously walked out to see what happened. We walked into the cheese factory. There was a big gapping hole in its roof. Underneath the hole, protruding from a huge black pot filled with molten cheese, the fins of an unexploded bomb stuck out.

Warsaw surrendered on September 27, 1939. We walked out into the street to a scene of destruction. It seemed there was hardly an undamaged structure left in the city. Countless buildings had huge holes ripped in their walls and roofs. Many were gutted. Beds and sinks hung crazily from upper floors. An eerie quiet settled over the city. Suddenly, while standing near the Gerbers' house, I heard a rhythmic sound of drums. In my childish thinking I imagined an approaching Boy Scout parade. Instead, rounding the corner was a column of helmeted, goose-stepping German soldiers. Thus began for me, and for my family, the dark period of the German occupation.

Return To Pruszków, 1939

After the fall of Warsaw, we returned to Pruszków. The town looked the same as before, but there was a dramatic change in its character. The streets were teeming with brown-and-black-shirted troopers wearing Nazi armbands. Some were ethnic Poles, but many were the so-called Volksdeutsche, Poles of German extraction, who lost no time stabbing their adopted country in

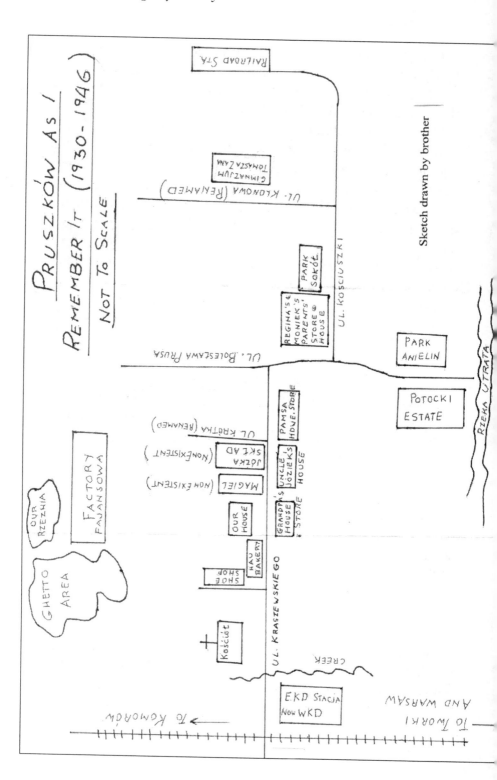

PRUSZKÓW AS I
REMEMBER IT (1930-1946)
NOT TO SCALE

Sketch drawn by brother

the back.

Initially we tried to lead our lives as before, but quickly it became apparent that the world we had known just one month earlier had dramatically changed. Polish youngsters and grownups looked at Jews with derision and open hostility. Hitler's screeching, maniacal voice blared from loudspeakers set up on the streets. Jerry and I were sheltered as much as possible from what was transpiring outside; much of what we knew we learned from overhearing the conversations of grownups. What we heard was depressing and worrying, even for youngsters our age. We learned that Jews had to wear armbands and were beaten up on the streets. We heard that Jews were being caught and shipped off for hard labor and that we had to step down from sidewalks when a German approached.

Mother's younger brother, Uncle Adam, had applied to study medicine in Warsaw, but was denied admission because he was Jewish. He then applied to a university in Czechoslovakia, where he successfully completed his degree. Shortly after our return to Pruszków, there was a knock on our Grandparents' door in the middle of the night. Uncle Adam was taken away without any explanation. Weeks and months filled with anxiety went by without any news from him. He just simply disappeared.

Our distress deepened when we heard that a similar thing had happened to the Gerber family in Warsaw, with the disappearance of the family member who worked in a bank. We did not realize it at that time, but both men were among the first victims of the Germans' early, country-wide, campaign to liquidate Jewish intellectuals. Uncle Adam was probably taken to a nearby forest and murdered there.

Even though he was a young man, Mother's oldest brother, Uncle Joziek, had a heart condition. He had his first heart attack before the war, and I recall that he was not allowed to carry anything heavier than one kilogram. At the beginning of the German occupation, he was caught and sent to the Majdanek death camp. In a letter he managed to smuggle out, he wrote that he was doing back-breaking labor loading coal onto railroad wagons. He died there, either of a heart attack or in one of

Majdanek's gas chambers. He served in the Polish army and years later I recognized him in his Polish army uniform in a photo in the Lochamey HaGetaot Museum in Israel.

Mother's middle brother, Uncle Rywek, managed to escape to the Soviet Union, where he survived the war years.

When the Polish army mobilized before the outbreak of the war, Jewish men were conscripted along with others to fight the German invader. Some 30,000 Jewish men died in battle. I remember attending a funeral in the Jewish cemetery in Pruszków and seeing the bodies of several Jewish soldiers wrapped in shrouds, awaiting burial. One of them was referred to as a hero. He had manned a machine-gun position, and had managed to hold off a column of advancing German soldiers for a long time.

The Ghetto In Pruszków, 1940

In 1940, Jews became increasingly persecuted in Pruszków. For a while we managed to maintain a reasonably dignified way of life, but it was getting difficult. The various discriminatory and humiliating decrees issued by the Germans, and the willing collaboration with them by a large part of the Polish population, began to take a toll. I remember hearing somber conversations of the grownups, conducted in subdued tones. There were no more social events, music or vacations. The routine of everyday life was disrupted and our thoughts were filled with dread. With every passing day the world around us seemed more threatening.

The culmination of this relentless process of discrimination was the establishment of a ghetto in Pruszków. I don't know precisely when our family received notice that we had to vacate our apartment and move into the ghetto, or when we actually moved there. Nor can I recall any activity in preparation for the move, such as packing boxes or suitcases. Perhaps we didn't pack anything. From what I recall, we were told, on short notice, to leave everything behind and move into the ghetto. I assume that Mother and Father managed to gather some things, although this time, no horse-drawn platforms were needed to move our belongings. The area designated for the ghetto was approximately two kilometers from our home and we, probably, walked there.

The ghetto was enclosed by a barbed-wire fence and its single gate was guarded by the Germans and the Polish police. The neighborhood was the poorest in town; the houses were old and dilapidated. Living conditions were dreadful. There was unbearable crowding with several families having been assigned to each apartment. Some basic food supplies were available. The Bienkowski family occasionally managed to smuggle a food basket into the ghetto for us. I marked my eighth birthday, October 18, 1940, in the Pruszków Ghetto. I don't recall this day being celebrated in any way, and neither were any of our other birthdays during the war years.

The Pruszków Ghetto was closed down after several months and we were deported to Warsaw. On the day of deportation, we were ordered to a large, empty lot and told to line up in rows. We stood there a long time. It was freezing cold. Jerry ended up with frost-bitten toes. People were carrying only small bundles; we were not allowed to take anything large with us. Valuables which could be hidden on our bodies, such as money and jewelry, were sewn into clothes and even hidden in women's intimate body parts. Father was not with us. When the deportation order arrived, he was taken, along with other men, to do forced labor at the railroad workshops in Pruszków.

A column of trucks, with tarpaulin roofs and open backs, rolled into the lot. Orders were barked. We climbed up and found a place to sit on a cold, wooden bench. The engines started. We began to move. Our destination: the Warsaw Ghetto.

For some 60 years I did not know the exact date on which we were deported, but I recently learned the date from "The Holocaust Chronicle," Publications International Ltd., P.216, which has the following entry: "*January 30, 1941: 3,000 deportees, mostly from the Polish town of Pruszków, arrive at the Warsaw Ghetto.*"

The Warsaw Ghetto; 1941

It was still daylight when we left Pruszków, but Polish winter nights descend rapidly, and by the time we reached Warsaw it was already dark. The trucks halted. On the command "Raus!" (Out), we climbed down from the truck.

We were marched off, escorted by armed Polish policemen. The streets were full of people. Occasionally a streetcar, its interior brightly lit and its bells ringing loudly, passed us. As on our visits to Warsaw before the war, I again found myself fascinated by the streetcars and I turned my head to watch them roll down the street. Apparently the policeman at my side noticed this, for he tapped me on the shoulder and said, "You will see plenty of them in paradise." To this day I wonder whether this was an expression of compassion or derision. I tend to think it was the latter.

When we arrived, the Warsaw Ghetto was already enclosed by a wall, but I do not recall seeing it or walking through one of its gates. The trucks, probably, deposited us inside the ghetto area. After walking for a while we were ushered into a low building which served as an assembly point for the deportees from the Warsaw district. The building was cold and crammed with people sitting on benches and on the floor. There was a strong smell of disinfectant. The walls were covered with posters in Polish and German admonishing people to keep clean, to beware of lice and to drink only boiled water. Many posters displayed human skulls with warnings against the dangers of the deadly typhus disease. I was then too young to grasp the cynicism of these posters, which preached hygiene to a population held in a state of starvation and sub-human living conditions.

My next recollection is of our apartment. In addition to the four of us, at first we shared our quarters with Grandfather Hanoch, Grandmother Henna and Grandfather Yakub Postolski, Uncle Joziek's wife, Mania, and their daughter Niusia. Eventually some of them found their own accommodations. My Grandfather Yakub and Grandmother Henna moved to an apartment on Prosta Street, a small street adjacent to ours.

Our apartment was located at the end of Pańska Street near the corner of Żelazna, very close to the ghetto wall. The wall left an indelible image in my memory, because it was just a few meters from our window and it blocked most of the daylight from our apartment. At night we often heard shots fired at Jews trying to climb over the wall in desperate efforts to smuggle some food for their starving families. Many of them were children my age. Smuggling was punishable by death. When caught, the "guilty" ones were executed on the spot.

What was the Warsaw Ghetto like? It's almost impossible to describe, but here are some facts. Before the war about 390,000 Jews lived in Warsaw. In 1940, they were evicted from their homes and ordered to move into the small, newly formed, ghetto area, thereby creating severely overcrowded living conditions. Between January and April 1941, the ghetto population swelled by an additional 150,000 people who were deported from neighboring towns. This resulted in unbearable crowding, with some 500,000 people squeezed into an area of about two square miles. On average, there were 13 people per room. Thousands were left homeless.[1]

The food allotment for Jews in the ghetto was 181 calories per day (in 1941 the official ration provided 2,613 calories per day for Germans living in Poland). Epidemics were rampant, particularly typhus, which was carried by lice. As a result, by the summer of 1942, only 18 months after the establishment of the ghetto, some 100,000 of its inhabitants had succumbed to disease and hunger. Undoubtedly, had it not been for the food-smuggling activity, this

---

1   Encyclopedia Judaica, Vol. 16, p.342.

number would have been much higher.[2]

Apparently, the original plan for the implementation of the "Final Solution of the Jewish Problem" was to kill the Jews in ghettos by starvation and disease. When this method proved to be too slow, the Wannsee Conference was convened in January, 1942. Different methods were discussed, with the aim of speeding up the killing process. The direct result of this conference was the establishment of a chain of death camps, whose sole purpose was to murder the maximum number of Jews in the minimum amount of time. One of these death camps, Treblinka, would probably have been where I would have been murdered if fate had not decreed otherwise.

Life In The Warsaw Ghetto

What was life like for me, an eight-year-old boy, while we lived in the Warsaw Ghetto? Did Jerry and I realize the seriousness of our situation? To a certain extent, yes, but, obviously, not as strong as the grownups must have felt it. They sheltered us, as much as possible, from the cruel reality surrounding us. I had complete confidence in our parents and instinctively trusted them to get us through any predicament, no matter how difficult.

Mother made no attempt to enroll us in a school in the ghetto. However, knowing our love of reading, she subscribed us

---

2   Friedlander, Saul, "The Years of Extermination," Chapter 2, p.105. "*In March 1941 the population density of the Warsaw Ghetto reached 1,309 persons per hundred square meters with an average of 7.2 persons sharing one room... These were average figures, for as many as 25 or even 30 people shared one room of 6 by 4 meters.*"

Chapter 3, p.147. From "The Information Bulletin of the Polish Underground" of March 1941, describing the conditions in the Warsaw Ghetto: "*Further crowding has resulted in ill-health, hunger and monstrous poverty that defy description. Groups of pale and emaciated people wander aimlessly through the overcrowded streets. Beggars sit and lie along the walls and the sight of people collapsing from starvation is common... contagious diseases are spreading, particularly tuberculosis.*"

Chapter 4, p. 243: "*In August, 1941...the monthly death rate in the ghetto was stabilizing at around 5,500 persons.*"

Map of the Warsaw Ghetto, 1940-43

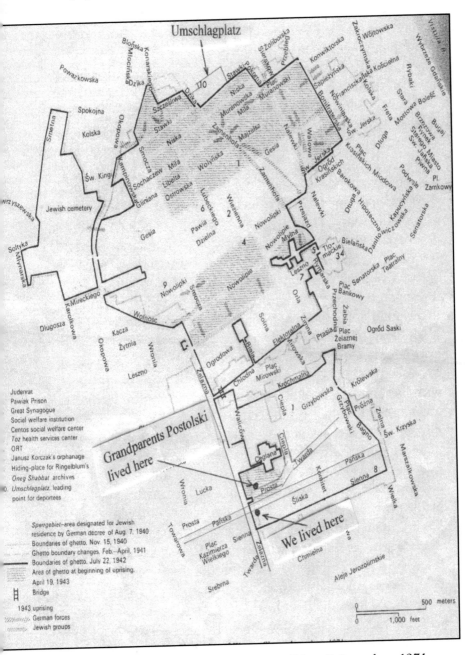

After J. Ziemian: "The Borders of Warsaw Ghetto", Jerusalem, 1971.
From Encyclopedia Judaica; Vol. 16; p. 347.

to a public library. I remember our walks there. The streets were thronged with milling crowds, newspapers were sold at numerous kiosks, and...human corpses lay on the sidewalks. Some of the bodies were covered with newspapers, but many were not, and from their appearance it was obvious they had died of starvation. The near-dead leaned against walls and held tin cans, begging for food or money.

How did all this affect me, a boy returning from a library with a book in his hand? At first the shock was enormous. But, with time it began to diminish. Death is a cruel blow to the human psyche. However, if a person is frequently faced with it and with its consequences, his emotional system appears to switch to a "self-defense" mode, which enables him to preserve his sanity. During the years of the Holocaust, death became such a constant companion that in many cases it lost its traumatic impact. We frequently received news that a relative or friend had been killed yet we managed to go on with our daily lives.

Apparently this was also the process that was then taking place in my mind. It enabled me to walk down a street strewn with dead bodies and then read a book or play with my brother. My eyes saw horror and death but my mind refused to let them destroy me.

We had enough to eat, but it was mostly watery cabbage soup with potatoes and bread. There were no dairy products, no fruit and no meat or fish on our table. When Mother called us for dinner, Jerry and I would jokingly line up in a row holding the plates in our hands. We kept after Mother, urging her to eat. We knew she was skimping on her food to give it to us.

One day a burly Polish man came to our apartment. From an inside pocket of his leather jacket he pulled out a whole sausage. He had smuggled it into the ghetto and came to try to sell it to us. A distinctive aroma, which only a Polish sausage can emit, filled the room. I inhaled deeply, absorbing with my whole hungry being the wonderful scent of meat and garlic.

Knowing how much we loved sausage, Mother tried to bargain with the man, but the price was high and he would not budge. After a while he stuffed the sausage back into his jacket and left.

When the door closed behind him, Mother, with tears in her eyes, explained to us that she, simply, could not afford to buy the sausage. Apparently, whatever assets she managed to smuggle out of Pruszków were slowly being exhausted. We understood, and in an effort to cheer her up, Jerry and I tried to make light of the whole incident.

Escape From The Warsaw Ghetto

The living conditions in the Warsaw Ghetto were so horrendous that I am certain we tried from the very beginning, to find some way to escape from it. I do not know how and when the escape was planned. Father was still in the forced labor camp in Pruszków. I don't know how he managed to communicate with us, but I am sure he had a part in the planning. I am also sure that the impetus for our escape came from a letter we received from our friends, the Zylbermans, who lived in the small town of Kosów Lacki, about 100 kilometers northeast of Warsaw. The Kosów area was also where our farm, Albinów, was located. (It was also where the Germans would soon build the Treblinka death camp.)

Our family and the Zylbermans probably became acquainted through common business interests. In time, a genuine friendship was forged. When we wrote to the Zylbermans about the hardships in the Warsaw Ghetto, we received a reply effectively saying, "Come to us. Our home will be your home."

We decided to take our chances with a man who made a dangerous living by smuggling Jews out of the ghetto. Of course, he was appropriately paid for his efforts, as were a number of other individuals who were bribed to look the other way or keep silent. I don't know what those payments were, but I recall hearing that the driver of a streetcar was bribed with a sack of potatoes. This may be hard to comprehend for someone who did not experience that period, and for whom the potato is just another vegetable. In those awful days, the possession of a potato frequently meant the difference between living and dying. Never mind that it was mostly starch; it filled the stomach with something edible, which was then just a dream for millions of starving people.

To make our escape, we relied on the streetcar. There was one streetcar line which originated in the Polish part of the city, crossed into the ghetto, and then returned to the Polish side. Jews were allowed to use this line only within the ghetto area, and had to disembark when the streetcar reached the ghetto boundary. At that point the streetcars were checked for any Jews who might have remained on board. Escape attempts from the ghetto were punishable by death.

One day, early in the morning, I found myself standing with Mother near streetcar tracks. A streetcar approached and halted. We quickly boarded through the door near the driver.

As soon as we entered, Mother ripped off the Star Of David armband she was wearing (I don't recall having to wear one). The driver kept looking straight ahead, pretending not to notice. Appearing as casual as possible, we sat down in seats in the front part of the car. Wearing my usual black beret, I sat down in the window seat and tried to look as bored as possible, though my nerves were tied in a knot. Mother sat in the aisle seat. The car halted. Two helmeted, armed German soldiers entered. I knew they were looking for Jews and if discovered, we might die. They slowly walked down the aisle, carefully checking every passenger for Semitic features. It was our turn. My heart beat wildly. The soldier first looked at Mother. He then began to scan my face and looked into my eyes. At that moment I felt myself breaking into a smile. The soldier smiled back and walked on. To this day, I don't know what prompted me to smile. I was frozen with fear. Was this some instinctive attempt at self-preservation? Did the smile help convince the soldier that I was not Jewish? I'll never know. The car proceeded and left the ghetto. We were safe!

I shudder at the thought of how easily our escape attempt could have ended in failure. At the time of our boarding, there were already passengers sitting in the car. As I entered, I avoided eye contact with them, and quickly sat down in my seat alongside Mother.

When the streetcar reached the ghetto boundary, the Jewish passengers got off and the non-Jewish ones remained and...so did we! When the soldiers came on board, all it would have taken to seal our fate was for one of the passengers point a finger at us and say "Żydy!" ("Jews"). We would have been taken off the car. My circumcision would have given us away. We would have been shot or, in the best case, beaten and returned to the ghetto. To those anonymous passengers who then remained silent, I wish to express my deepest gratitude.

The next day, Jerry and Grandfather Hanoch successfully repeated this streetcar maneuver. To get to Kosów, we walked and took a train part of the way (again posing as gentiles, since Jews were forbidden to use public transportation).

I am not sure exactly when Father arrived in Kosów. He escaped from the railroad works in Pruszków and walked the distance of some 100 kilometers to join us. Our joy was boundless. From that day on, we were able to stay together throughout the war years.

Our farm, Albinów, was just a few kilometers from Kosów. Being the rightful owners of this place, we hoped to get some assistance from there. But we hoped in vain. By the time we arrived, the Germans had already confiscated the property and appointed a Polish administrator to manage it. I remember the day when Father returned from Albinów with the sad news that we cannot expect any help from there.

In Kosów Lacki

The Zylberman family, like ours, numbered five: parents, two children and a grandfather. The father, David Zylberman, was a tall, lanky, suntanned man who usually wore a flat-beaked peasants' cap. He radiated physical strength and stamina. I remember his strong hands cutting bread at our meals. Mrs. Zylberman was short and plump with many pock-marks on her face. She had a warm personality and an ever-ready smile. It is her smile which I remember well, since, while smiling, she would expose a mouth full of gold teeth.

The Zylbermans' son, nicknamed Bumek, was about a year older than Jerry, and like Jerry was an avid stamp collector. They loved to trade stamps, and I remember hearing them say things like, "I'll give you the one with Hitler for the one with the Russian soldiers."

Mala, the Zylbermans' daughter, was about a year older than I. She had a large red spot on one of her cheeks, dating from the time she overturned a burning kerosene lamp on herself. What made her unforgettable for me was her love of singing. She taught me some Polish songs which I remember to this day.

The Zylbermans had a dog named Zuch (pronounced 'Zookh') meaning "Brave." He was small, white, with clipped ears and a short tail. He was our faithful companion at play and enjoyed walking with us in the fields. One day Bumek asked me to point my index finger at him. I did, and I was startled to see this lovely, cuddly dog turning into a snarling beast. He exposed a set of threatening fangs and his eyes shot green rays of fury. He growled deeply and leaned back, ready to lunge at me. Astonished, I

The Zylberman Family Tree

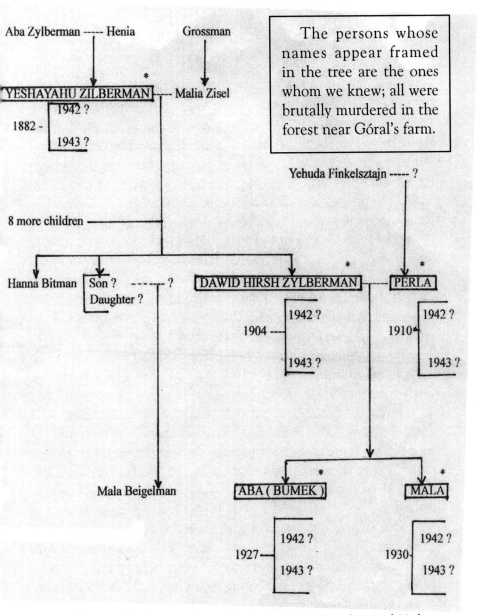

The persons whose names appear framed in the tree are the ones whom we knew; all were brutally murdered in the forest near Góral's farm.

The Zylberman family tree, drawn by the author, is based on Yad Vashem pages of testimony written by Hanna Bitman, David Zylberman's sister and Mala Beigelman, Bumek's and Mala's cousin.

quickly lowered my hand and watched him gradually return to his former demeanor. Bumek, obviously amused by my startled reaction, laughingly explained, "He was protecting me. He saw soldiers shoot puppies and he thought your finger was a gun you were pointing at me."

Zuch had another curious habit. Five days a week he ate anything and everything that was shoved his way. At mealtimes he sat patiently and waited for scraps, which he eagerly devoured. However, beginning Friday evening and all through Saturday, the Sabbath, he touched nothing but challah, the traditional braided Sabbath bread. When Bumek first told me of this, I didn't believe it. But one Sabbath I offered Zuch a slice of regular bread. He would not take it. In disdain he turned his head away from me, but then eagerly pounced on a slice of challah I held out to him.

In 1941, about half of Kosów's 2,000 inhabitants were Jewish. The Polish residents were mostly farmers who eked out a living from small plots of land. Many of them owned only one horse, one cow, and one or two pigs. They tilled the land with horse-drawn plows and mowed the crops with scythes. They grew mostly wheat, rye and barley and produced enough hay to feed their livestock. The Jewish population consisted mainly of small craftsmen, such as shoemakers, tailors and carpenters. Some, like the Zylbermans, worked and traded in agriculture.

The Zylbermans' home was a typical Kosów dwelling. The entrance to the home led directly from the street into a small room. Here, there stood a simple table with chairs, a clothes closet, and a few other pieces of furniture. We ate in this room. To the right a door led into a small kitchen, where cooking and baking were done on a wood-fed stove. To the left a door led into the bedroom, small and crowded with beds and another clothes closet. The house was lit with kerosene lamps. Water was drawn from a hand-operated pump in the yard. To the right of the entrance from the street, was a door leading into a toilet. (I don't remember seeing any flushing provisions.)

Into this, already-crowded situation, the arrival of the five of us made the living conditions that much more difficult. For the night, field-beds were set up all over the house. We, the four children, slept in two of these beds, lying in a head-to-toe fashion. I was told to sleep with Mala, and I remember how hurt my feelings were. Imagine, I, a boy almost nine years old, having to sleep with a girl!

After the hellish Warsaw Ghetto, Kosów seemed like paradise. True, Jews there were occasionally harassed and beaten on the streets. But this did not compare to the insufferable conditions under which Jews were forced to live in the various, recently created, ghettos throughout Poland. The letters we received from our family, who remained in the Warsaw Ghetto, when read between lines, hinted strongly at their increasingly desperate situation. In contrast, the food in Kosów was plentiful and Jews were allowed to continue living in their homes and freely move about town.

Jewish children were forbidden to attend school. We had no contact with gentile children or, for that matter, with any children at all. Jerry was occasionally sent to work (for no wages) in a Jewish-owned carpenter shop, not so much to learn the trade but rather to keep him busy.

I don't remember reading books or playing games while living in Kosów. Instead of playing with toys, I fantasized to fill the emptiness of my childhood. In my mind, a stone became a house, blades of grass turned into a forest and a piece of wood became a train.

We played with Zuch and the Zylberman children, ran in the fields, and tried to make ourselves useful in the house. Jerry helped with farm chores and I, sometimes, tended to the cows. I herded them barefoot, with stick in hand, in a nearby meadow. The ground was richly carpeted with grass with a sprinkling of daffodils. I enjoyed those direct encounters with nature. Mother helped with household chores and Father assisted Mr. Zylberman in his business.

The German-Russo War, 1941
The border between the German- and Russian-occupied zones

of Poland lay just east of Kosów, along the river Bug. In the spring of 1941, we became aware of a steadily increasing German military presence in Kosów. Columns of tanks, some almost as high as the residential homes, moved down the streets, their treads ripping up the unpaved surface and raising clouds of dust. Motorcycles manned by helmeted, goggled soldiers and troop-carrying trucks roared by.

The Germans attacked early in the morning of June 22, 1941. We were still sleeping when a tremendous explosion almost threw me out of bed. I opened my eyes and saw Mother run into the room. She grabbed me. We ran out to a nearby field where we dived into a ditch. Fearful, we listened to the explosions of bombs and artillery fire, undoubtedly sounds of a raging front line battle. At first, the sounds were strong but they quickly diminished. Eventually, silence returned, interrupted only by frequent overflights of German aircraft.

Heaving sighs of relief, we returned home. Had we known, at that time, the significance of what had just occurred, and the impact it would have on our lives, our relief would quickly change to a feeling of anxiety and fear. O, how we yearned, in the years to come, to again hear the roar of a front line battle!

Within days, the streets of Kosów became filled with thousands of exhausted, ragged Russian prisoners being herded by German soldiers with bayonets fixed on their rifles. Faces smudged, heads bound with bloodied bandages, limping on crutches and leaning on sticks, the prisoners passed us in a stupor. They were obviously starving. Any attempts by bystanders to hand them bread or water, were roughly rebuffed by the soldiers. Some weeks later we saw trucks filled with their corpses passing by. The trucks were not covered. I remember seeing limp legs and arms hanging over the sides. Some of the corpses had missing buttocks, indicating possible cannibalism.

1942

In 1942, in the far-off Wannsee suburb of Berlin, top German officials held a conference. The purpose of this meeting was to expedite the extermination of European Jews. As its plans were being implemented, we in Kosów began to feel its consequences. Increasingly more Kosów Jews were being randomly apprehended on the streets and sent off to do forced labor. Many were sent to work in a forest near a small village called Treblinka some 12 kilometers north of Kosów. A small prisoner-of-war camp for Russian soldiers, captured in 1941, had been located at that site. In 1942 the Germans had completely redesigned and greatly enlarged it for an as yet unknown purpose.

The harassment of Jews on the streets intensified. One day Grandfather Hanoch entered the house shaken and out of breath, with the dog Zuch following him. He told us that while he was walking down the street, a German soldier suddenly grabbed him by the arm and started to drag him away. Zuch jumped up and sank his teeth into the soldier's hand. The soldier shrieked in pain, released Grandfather, and with a drawn bayonet began to chase the dog. Grandfather ran off in one direction and Zuch in another (this incident was witnessed by Jerry). Both Grandfather and Zuch managed to reach home safely. Zuch was indeed "brave" as his name implied.

It was only later that we understood why the Jews of Kosów were treated for so long with a "gentler glove" than Jews in other communities. The reason was that Kosów was a convenient source of Jewish labor for the construction of the nearby Treblinka death camp. Jews were being forced to construct with their own hands a facility designed to kill them, this in accordance with the nefarious German system of murder, in which the intended victims were forced to prepare their own executions. The guiding principle was that as little effort as possible was to be expended by the German "Herrenvolk" and their Slav collaborators in the killing process.

In the death camps, Jews were forced to clean the gas chambers after every gassing and then burn the corpses. In mass executions, Jews were forced to dig their own graves, and when the shooting ended, other Jews were made to cover the graves and then dig their own. Jews were made to organize their so-called Councils (known as Judenräte) to spare the Germans the messy bureaucratic effort of providing victims for the death transports.

It was for this reason that the Jews of Kosów were kept alive long after the liquidation of numerous Jewish communities throughout Poland. Thus, the first "aktzyah" (action, operation or round-up) in Kosów took place a full two months after the beginning of the deportations from Warsaw Ghetto to Treblinka. The Germans must have known that some of the Kosów Jews would try to escape, but they also knew that these Jews had no place to run. If discovered, the hostile Polish population would either denounce them or murder them on the spot.

Some events which have remained engraved in my memory are clearly connected to the deportation of Jews from the Warsaw Ghetto to Treblinka. One day an unexpected visitor came to us in Kosów. He was from Pruszków, and had been sent from there to the Warsaw Ghetto, as we had been. When the deportations to Treblinka began, he was taken to the Umschlagplatz (the assembly point and station from which the death trains left) and shoved into a cattle car. On the way to Treblinka he jumped from the moving train. A Ukrainian guard fired at him, the bullet grazing his forehead. Knowing where we were, he made his way to Kosów. We bandaged his bleeding head.

"Where was the train heading?" we asked.

"There is a place near here called Treblinka. People say they kill Jews there," he answered. Treblinka…! By now this name had acquired a sinister meaning. In time the word Treblinka would become synonymous with death.

One day, another man from Pruszków came to our door. I remember sitting with others around a table listening to him. Horrified, we sat in silence as he told his story. He, his wife, and their five-year-old daughter had been taken to the Umschlagplatz in the Warsaw Ghetto. It was a hot day. The cattle car into which they were ordered was jammed with people.

Their little girl constantly cried and begged for something to drink. What I remember from that evening is not the man's features or his clothes, but just a few words he said. In a low, shy voice he said, "I gave her my urine to drink." I had no idea what happened to this man and his family.[1]

As the summer of 1942 passed, the news which reached us in Kosów became progressively more alarming. The word I began to hear more and more frequently was "akcja" (pronounced "aktzyah"). I understood that this word stood for an event which was life-threatening to us, Jews, and in which, most likely, we would die. Neighboring towns and villages, usually at night, were being suddenly surrounded by Germans, along with Ukrainians and the Polish police. The Jews were being driven out of their homes without being allowed to take anything with them. Some were shot on the spot; others were beaten and murdered by local Poles. The remaining ones were then assembled in some central point in town, led to a waiting train, shoved into cattle cars and taken somewhere.

"To where?" we kept asking. Could it be that the rumors we

---

1   Twenty-nine years later, at a memorial ceremony for the Pruszków victims held in Haifa, Israel, a small, thin man wearing a hat approached me.

"Do you know who I am?" he asked. I had no idea.

I am the man who jumped from a train with my family and came to you in Kosów."

I stood speechless. As years and then decades had rolled by, I sometimes asked myself whether the things I thought I remembered actually happened. Maybe that evening in Kosów was just a figment of my imagination? But here, in front of me, stood a flesh-and-blood human being whose very presence said to me: "Yes. All this happened. You did not just imagine it!"

We sat down and he, briefly, told me again what I must have already heard then in Kosów so many years ago – how he had, with superhuman effort, thrown his wife and daughter out of the train and then jumped after them; how they were shot at, but luckily not hit. He knew that we were in Kosów, he said, and so, having left his family in a forest, came to see us. As he talked, I listened wordlessly to this man who so abruptly thrust the past into my present life. He must have sensed what effect his sudden appearance had on me.

"Would you like to meet my family?" he asked.

I walked over to meet his wife, now a grandmotherly-looking woman. At her side sat a young woman – their daughter – and next to her a small girl, about the same age as her mother was when her grandfather threw her out of a train headed for Treblinka.

were hearing about Treblinka were true? Could it be that Jews were being taken there to be put to death?

I doubt whether at that time my parents, or anyone else, knew the truth. For quite some time, even as the killings in Treblinka were already in full swing, the Germans managed to keep the activity a secret.

How did they do it? The method was simple. A Jew who crossed Treblinka's three-meter-high fence never came out to tell the story. The average life-span of a Jew in Treblinka was about two hours. However, despite this tight secrecy, rumors that something terrible was going on in Treblinka began to spread. With time, we became convinced that near that tiny, neighboring village of Treblinka, a monstrous killing machine had been put into action.

Some time in 1942, two events took place which, I later realized, critically affected our chances of survival. The first was the death of Grandfather Hanoch. I remember walking with my family along a sandy path behind a horse-drawn wagon carrying his casket. The cemetery was small and unimposing and the ceremony was brief.

Had Grandfather continued to live, we would, surely, have been discovered in our hiding place. There our lives depended on our ability to maintain complete silence. Grandfather suffered from prolonged bouts of a dry, chronic, cough, which would have given us away. Thus, I have no doubt that with his death, Grandfather granted us life. Sadly, during the Holocaust, one person's demise, sometimes, increased the chances of another person's survival.

The second event, critical to our survival, was that Father managed to recover from a bout of typhus. This dreadful, debilitating disease claimed the lives of millions during the war years. Father recovered, although he lost most of his hair and much weight. Had he died, we certainly would have perished later on. It was his stubborn optimism and boundless energy which enabled us to survive. Without him we would never have found a place to hide, and probably would have been murdered in Treblinka with all the other Jews of Kosów. And so, in Father's case, his remaining alive granted us life.

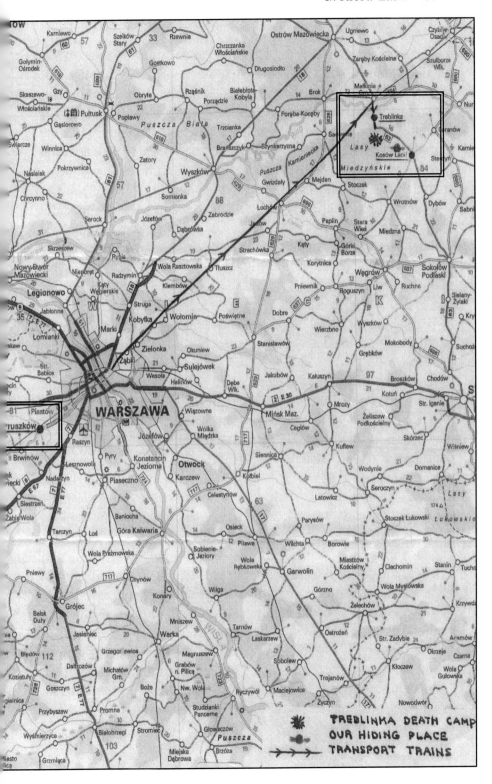

TREBLINKA DEATH CAMP
OUR HIDING PLACE
TRANSPORT TRAINS

As the summer wore on, Jerry and I and the Zylberman children talked among ourselves about what we thought was taking place. It was inevitable that the worry we saw in the faces of our parents would affect us. But, being children, we dealt with fear by spinning fantasies. We planned to surprise our parents by building a hideout in a nearby field. I remember what the shelter was to be like. It was to be built of straw with wooden beams, and it eerily resembled the one we actually entered some two months later. We planned to keep the existence of this hideout a secret until the moment when the aktzyah actually began. Then we would break the good news to our parents that they have nothing to worry about since our shelter was ready to save both of our families.

The Aktzyah In Kosów

As time passed, we heard of aktzyahs taking place in neighboring villages. It must have become obvious to my parents, to the Zylbermans, and to all Jews in town, that it was only a matter of time before Kosów's turn came. But I was not aware that we were making any preparations to meet this fast-approaching danger.

One late evening we were sitting around the table. Father was not with us. It was late, but we were fully dressed. People around me spoke in low voices. There were strong rumors that something might happen that night. I sensed the tension in the air. It was hot in the room and I was drowsy. Suddenly the door tore open. A man with a wild look on his face stepped in, screamed the dreaded word "Niemcy!" ("Germans!"), and disappeared.

An indescribable panic ensued. Mother grabbed my arm and jerked me out of the chair. We ran outside. Upon stepping out of the door, we turned sharply to the left and ran into the yard. It was pitch dark. I could barely make out the outlines of the barn ahead of us and of the warehouse on our right.

"Where to? Where to?" I cried, but Mother did not answer and just kept pulling me along with her. We ran to the end of the warehouse, turned the corner and stopped. My heart pounded wildly; I was out of breath. I saw someone bend down and pull a stone out of the foundation of the warehouse. One by one we crawled inside and someone replaced the stone. It was pitch black. At first I could not see anything. When my vision returned, I slowly managed to turn over so that I was lying on my back. We were under the floor of the warehouse, the wooden boards just a few inches from my face. I don't know how long we lay there, motionless and in absolute silence.

Suddenly the gate of the warehouse creaked. Mother raised a finger to her mouth to signal me to keep silent. I was paralyzed with fear and could not have spoken, even had I wanted to. Some people entered the warehouse and were walking above us; I saw the floor above my face bend under their weight. I heard voices and held my breath. They were speaking Polish and laughing while they turned over sacks of grain looking for Jews. Again and again I heard the thumping sound of sacks being thrown on the floor. After some time we again heard the creaking of the gate as it was being closed. We remained silent and motionless for a long time, fearing that someone might still be in the warehouse. Throughout the night we heard people shouting and shots being fired.

At dawn, light began filtering in through the cracks in the foundation. I am almost certain that Mother gave me something to eat. Whoever had planned our shelter saw to it that we had some place to relieve ourselves. By sliding on my belly to a small depression dug out in the ground, I was able to empty my bladder, but only with great difficulty.

We continued to hear sporadic shooting throughout the next day. Suddenly we heard someone shouting outside. I did not understand what he was saying. Mother whispered to me that it was Father. He had been caught on the street, and was put on a detail to carry dead bodies to the cemetery. He made it a point to come as close as possible to our hideout. By shouting, he let us know that he was alive. Mother told me that he shouted in Yiddish, "Oyfin gitn ort!" which means "at the cemetery." Later she told us that at that moment she thought he was being led to the cemetery to be executed.

I don't remember how we learned that the aktzyah had ended. Perhaps we heard no more shots or cries, or perhaps Father came to get us. After three days under the floor of the warehouse, the stone in the foundation was removed and we slowly crawled out into the open.

Other survivors told us that the Jews of Kosów were rounded up and marched off to the town's main square. What happened to them? For 65 years I assumed that they, like those in other towns, were sent by train to Treblinka. They were indeed sent to Treblinka, but not by train. Recently, while researching the subject, I came across an article[2] written by someone who visited Treblinka in 2003. It was from this article that I learned for the first time the date of the aktzyah in Kosów. The three days we spent under the floor of a warehouse were September 22, 23 and 24, 1942.

This article further deepens the trauma I feel whenever the subject of Treblinka comes up. Reading these words I shudder at the thought of the fate that awaited us had we not found a place to hide. We would have been forced to march 12 kilometers to be murdered! We probably would not have had any food or drink. And so, hungry, thirsty, broken both physically and emotionally, we would have marched along that "serene, narrow, black road" to our deaths in the gas chambers of Treblinka.

As it turned out, the Jews of Kosów Lacki proved to be quite

2   Yad Vashem Archives: 03/3304; Central Zionist Archives: Z4/3003-IV: Kosów Lacki Jews were a source of slave laborers that built and enlarged the extermination camp Treblinka, a mere 12 kilometers northeast of Kosów, from a small Soviet POW camp to a super efficient death camp for Jews. During the three days of 22-25 September 1942, the 1,200 Kosów Ghetto residents and refugees were marched by foot on the narrow bent country side road between Kosów Lacki and Treblinka. They were the only death transport to arrive at the gates of Treblinka by foot. All other transports arrived by train. All of the Kosów Jews were exterminated promptly upon arrival.

The road looks today (August 2003) the same as it looked in September 1942. Same birch trees along the road, same wide fields spreading to the horizon, same Mother Mary icons at the entrance to the scarce Polish villages along the road. If you ever drive on this Polish country forsaken road on your visit to Treblinka, stop the car and walk for a while on this serene, narrow black strip segment that connects the shtetl of Kosów Lacki with Treblinka, and follow the path of the one and only foot death transport to Treblinka.

"cost-efficient" for the Germans. While they were alive, they provided them with slave labor, and on the way to die they even spared the Germans the need to provide transportation. When Kosów Lacki's Jews appeared at Treblinka's gates, Kurt Franz, the commandant, that flunky waiter from a small Bavarian town turned mass killer, must have been very pleased with himself.

After The Aktzyah

After we emerged from our hideout under the warehouse, our family was led, with other survivors, to a section of Kosów which was unfamiliar to me. This area had been home to those who provided services for the rest of the population. Here were small streets where tailors, carpenters and other craftsmen practiced their trades. This was where, until only a few days earlier, most of the Jewish residents of Kosów had lived.

I shall never forget the scene of destruction and desolation we saw here. It looked as though it had been hit by a vicious storm. It was a ghost town. In those fateful three days of the aktzyah, all of Kosów's Jews had been rounded up, beaten and driven on foot to die in Treblinka. In street after street houses stood empty, their windows broken, their open doors flapping in the wind. The streets were littered with pieces of furniture, open drawers, fragments of clothing and broken glass. But, above all, what is forever etched in my memory, are the mounds of paper, documents and hundreds of photographs lying scattered in the street.

This was not the work of the Germans. This havoc was wreaked by local Poles. The demise of the Jews gave them the opportunity to pillage and loot their property.

This area was to be our new home. Soon we were joined by survivors of the aktzyahs which took place in neighboring towns. It became obvious that the German plan was to concentrate all the survivors in one place, where they could easily be rounded up and liquidated at a later time. Those who survived the first aktzyah would be caught in the second one, and perhaps, in yet another one until Kosów and the surrounding area were "Judenrein" – cleansed of Jews.

Life in this newly-formed Kosów ghetto was a daily nightmare. Someone would shout "Niemcy!" and waves of indescribable panic engulfed every man, woman and child. There were frantic, hysterical shouts. Sobbing parents looked for their children. Children desperately cried for their parents. Everybody tried to find some shelter – any place to hide. Some closed themselves in clothes closets, others crawled under beds. Our family no longer had a warehouse to hide under. Again and again we were swept up in those frenzied, nerve-draining waves of panic (in one of them I was stuffed into a clothes closet).

Apparently the Germans were planning another aktzyah in Kosów in the near future, because they did not bother to put up a wall, or even a fence around the area of this new ghetto. Ironically, this almost cost me my life.

I was ten years old. Like other children my age, I enjoyed walking with a stick and kicking pebbles. One day I was particularly absorbed in this pastime, stopping at times to pick up one of the photographs lying in the street. Most of the photographs showed smiling, happy people dressed in festive clothes gathered around tables. I thought about taking some of the pictures with me and starting a collection. However, the thought that these people were now dead, made me put the pictures back where I found them.

At some point, as I aimlessly walked the streets of our wall-less ghetto, I sensed that something was wrong. Maybe the images I saw out of the corners of my eyes changed, or maybe there were no more photographs lying on the ground. Suddenly I realized that I had strayed outside the boundaries of the ghetto. I knew that any Jew caught outside the ghetto area would be executed on the spot.

Before I could make a dash back into the ghetto, I heard the sound of clacking hoofs. A doroshka (a horse-drawn cab) turned the corner. It was coming straight toward me. In the backseat sat two SS officers in spotless uniforms and shining boots with their pistols at their sides. My heart froze. For a moment I hoped that they would not notice me. Then, one of the officers turned his head and his eyes fell on mine. I shall never forget those blue eyes in that fair-skinned face. Without lowering his eyes, the officer nudged his friend and pointed at me. The doroshka was now so close I could almost touch it. I stood rooted to the spot, fighting with all my strength the urge to run. He kept looking at me and I at him. Then, probably because I did not know what else to do, I began to smile. They burst out laughing, and were still laughing when the doroshka passed me and disappeared around the corner.

For the second time in my short life, I may have been saved by an involuntary, instinctive smile.

I ran back to the ghetto. I knew who those officers were. They were from nearby Treblinka. Death rode in that doroshka, and I had looked in its eyes.

Into Hiding

The aktzyah in Kosów shattered any illusions we may have had about what was in store for us. The Germans could easily have liquidated all the survivors who returned to Kosów from the surrounding fields and forests and other hiding places. They chose not to do it. Apparently such hasty action did not fit into their master plan and they decided to let us live a bit longer. Perhaps it was not possible, at that time, to squeeze us into Treblinka's "busy schedule" (at that time as many as 18,000 Jews were being killed there daily…!) Whatever the reason, we were granted a short reprieve in this nightmarish cat-and-mouse game. Mother and Father must have realized that unless we made some attempt to save ourselves, our days were numbered. Our choice was: make a move and we might live, or do nothing and we would surely die.

As a ten-year-old, was I aware of this grim choice we had to make? Even though I lived in a world of constant fear and sudden panic, in which we frantically rushed to find shelter, my mind refused to consider the possibility that I might actually die. No doubt, this had much to do with the confidence I had in my parents' ability to see us through any situation, no matter how dangerous. Had I known then how many Jewish parents were trying in vain to save their children, how many were trying to shield them with their bodies at the edges of execution pits, how many were trying to save them with their last, gasping breath in the gas chambers – had I known all this, I certainly would have despaired and lost all hope.

But hadn't my parents gotten us out alive from the siege of

Warsaw and from the Warsaw Ghetto? Hadn't they saved our lives in the aktzyah in Kosów? And so, my childish reasoning gave me hope that now, too, they would find some way for us to survive. (I recall only one instance in which this faith I had in my parents was shaken. We were out in a field and saw a group of armed men with dogs approaching. I was sure that I was going to die within the next few minutes. I broke down in sobs. I felt an immense wave of anger sweeping over me – anger at the Germans, at the Poles, at the whole world and…at my parents whom I, at that moment, blamed for getting us into this situation. Fortunately we were not harmed, but to this day I feel guilty for having bitterly shouted at my parents, "Why did you do this to us?")

One day I became aware that plans were being made to escape from the Kosów ghetto. From the bits of conversations I overheard between Mother and Father and Mr. Zylberman, I learned that the Zylbermans had found a Polish farmer in the vicinity of Kosów who was willing to hide them.

I don't know how the Zylbermans survived the aktzyah. The most logical place for them to have hidden was under their own warehouse with us. They, most likely, were there but I don't recall seeing them. Surely Zuch could not have been hiding with us under the warehouse for his barking would have given us away. And yet he was alive after the aktzyah, as was the whole Zylberman family.

My parents enlisted the help of two brothers, Mendel and Abram Rzepka (pronounced Zhepka) to find a farmer willing to hide our family. The reward the brothers were promised was that we would take them with us into hiding.

The Rzepka brothers' efforts were successful. They found a farmer, named Jan Góral, who agreed to hide us on his farm. We escaped from the Kosów ghetto, I estimate, some time in October 1942.

We walked out of the Kosów Lacki ghetto on a clear, cold night. The conditions for escape were far from ideal. The sky was studded with stars and the ground was covered with a deep layer of snow. We left tracks which could have been easily followed.

With every step it was becoming more difficult for me to get my legs out of the snow. I had no idea then to where, and in what direction we were heading.

Years later I came to the conclusion that we were then heading north...in the direction of Treblinka...! It was as if that black hole of Treblinka kept, physically, pulling us toward it – from our hometown eastward to Warsaw, from there northeastward to Kosów Lacki, and then northward...ever closer to its murderous core, ever closer to its abyss of horror...we stopped at its edge!

We reached Góral's farm late in the evening. I was exhausted. Since the shelter under the barn, where we were to hide, had not yet been dug, we found temporary shelter in a loft above a cow shed.

The shelter was to be dug out by Father and the Rzepka brothers, with the Góral family's assistance. But, apparently, there were some important things we did not bring with us from the ghetto. Soon after our arrival, Father and the Rzepkas decided to return to Kosów. They set out in the middle of the night.

We had just settled down for the night on the bales of hay in the loft when suddenly we heard sporadic shooting. The sharp, clapping sounds reverberated in the still night air. We were terrified. Had we been followed? Perhaps Father and the Rzepkas were caught and shot? We heard someone climbing up the ladder. Góral's head popped up through the opening, his eyes wide with fear.

"Quick!" he yelled. "Come down and run into the forest!"

Gripped by panic, we raced down the ladder into the cold night. Ahead of us we could see the outline of a forest. We ran toward it with all our remaining strength. We entered the forest. Moonlight filtered in through the branches. The ground was covered with snow. We found a tree with relatively little snow around it and crouched under it. We did not utter a word. There was absolute silence around us – no breeze to rustle the trees, no cries of birds, no sounds of insects – everything seemed frozen into immobility by the dreadful cold of a Polish winter night.

I don't know how long we sat there; it might have been hours.

I simply lost track of time. Mother kept falling asleep. Father used to warn us to never fall asleep in freezing weather for we might never wake up. So now, whenever we saw Mother's eyes closing or her head nodding, Jerry and I nudged her and whispered in her ears. We must have been wearing some reasonably warm clothing, but after a while I began to shiver. I was filled with terror at the thought of being discovered by Germans or by the local Poles (which in either case would have spelled the end of our lives) and worry about Father's fate.

Suddenly we heard steps crunching the snow. Someone was walking in the forest. We hardly dared to breathe. Then we heard a faint whistle – a pattern of sounds frequently used by Jerry. Carefully, Jerry whistled in return, using the same sounds. Then we heard another whistle, and another, and yet another, each one coming closer. Suddenly, between the trees, we saw Father and the Rzepkas approaching us. That frightful winter night in the Polish forest had come to an end. We walked back to Góral's farm. (Later we learned that the shots we heard were being fired by the crew of a German airplane which had crash-landed nearby. Some of the crew had gone to Kosów to seek help. On their way back they got lost. The shots were fired to help them find their way back to the airplane.)

It took several days to dig the shelter under the barn. The work had to be done under the cover of darkness. The dirt was carried out in buckets and spread out in the fields, so as not to arouse suspicion. We spent those days on the bundles of hay in the loft above the cow shed.

Our main wish at that time was to make ourselves invisible to the world. In this respect the Góral farm was nearly ideal. It was located in the middle of a wide expanse of pastures and tilled land and it had no close neighbors. Except for the nearby forest, all around the farm lay extensive fields dotted with clumps of trees. I remember seeing paths leading from the farm to somewhere, presumably to some neighboring farms, but I don't recall seeing any houses on the horizon.

In The Barn – The Eleven Of Us

There were six of us on that evening in October 1942, when we first entered the shelter: our family of four and the two brothers, Mendel and Abram Rzepka. On the day of liberation there were 11 of us. How did it happen that our number almost doubled, and who were the people who joined us in hiding?

Mendel Rzepka was about 20 years old and his brother, Abram, was about 17. Their entire family had been murdered in the Kosów aktzyah; they were the only survivors. Mendel was of medium height, sturdily built and had blonde hair. Abram was slender, with a thin, pale face and dark hair. They belonged to some Zionist youth movement, and often spoke of the longing of the Jewish people to return to Palestine, their ancestral homeland. I remember them saying, "The Jewish people must have a country of its own!" Although I came from a strongly Zionist home, this was the first time I had heard anyone make such an emphatic statement about the Jewish people and Palestine. Their words planted seeds in the mind of a 10-year-old boy who, because he was Jewish, had been, already for three years, forced to run for his life. (For the past 41 years, I am a proud citizen of a Jewish state – the State of Israel.)

Mendel Rzepka was devoted to his younger brother and very protective of him. On one occasion Abram fell ill. After a few days Mendel curtly informed us that after dark he intended to go to Kosów to get some medicine for him. This worried us; we were afraid that Mendel might get caught and, under torture, disclose where we were hiding. We tried to talk him out of it, but he suddenly became angry, got up, climbed the ladder and disappeared. There was nothing we could do except sit and worry. Some hours later he returned with the medicine. He told us that he woke the pharmacist in Kosów by knocking on his bedroom window. The risks he took that evening for himself, and for all of us, were enormous. Apparently his love for his brother overruled all considerations. After a few days of taking the medicine, Abram recovered.

Soon after we entered the shelter we were joined by a woman named Gitel and her daughter, Feige. Gitel was probably in her mid-forties; she had a somewhat wrinkled face, blue eyes and short dark hair sprinkled with gray. With their arrival, our number in the shelter rose to eight.

Somewhat later three men joined us. They were escapees from Treblinka. I recall the names of only two of them: Shimon, a wagon driver, whose favorite subject was horses, and Berl, who had a bushy moustache resembling my Grandfather's. (Berl had a weakness for drink, and this addiction would, eventually, prove fatal for him and affect the lives of others.) I don't remember the name of the third man, but I recall he came from Warsaw, was bald and rather heavily built, had a slightly hooked nose, and was, apparently, quite knowledgeable about life's delights. He entertained us with stories which were unsuitable for young boys to hear. I saw Mother and Father squirm whenever he embarked on one of them. Once, in the middle of such a story, I asked, "What is the meaning of prostytutka?" From the amused smiles around me, and the looks on my parents' faces, I surmised that I asked something inappropriate. Needless to say, my question was not answered.

The arrival of these five individuals in our shelter raises many questions in my mind. They can, probably, never be answered. Were their arrivals pre-arranged? Were they expected? How did Gitel and Feige, and the three men, know where we were hiding? Did any of us venture into Kosów to bring Gitel and Feige to the farm? Did the three men escape from the camp known as Treblinka One or from Treblinka Two? (Treblinka One was a penal, forced-labor camp mainly for Poles, but there were also Jews confined there. Some 10,000 prisoners died there from starvation, beatings and back-breaking labor. Treblinka Two was the death camp where the mass killing of Jews took place; an estimated 850,000 died there. In an uprising which took place in Treblinka Two on August 3, 1943, about 600 prisoners broke through the fence, but only 40 survived the war. Most of the escapees were hunted down by the Germans with the active help of the local Polish population.)

When Feige arrived she was already a married woman. Her husband's name was Ruven. However, Feige came to us only with her mother. Where then was Ruven?

Before Gitel and Feige's escape from Kosów, Ruven had been caught on the street and sent to Treblinka. He was in Treblinka with the three men who joined us in the shelter. (This makes it probable that all four of them were in Treblinka One, since in Treblinka Two the life expectancy of a Jew was measured in hours.) It's likely that before he was caught, Ruven had made contact with Father. He may have known Father from the past, or maybe he came to know him through the Zylbermans. Apparently he knew about the Górals and he probably offered Father money to take him, Gitel and Feige into hiding with us. He must have told Gitel and Feige about it, and that is how the two women found their way to Góral's farm.

I remember the day the three Treblinka escapees came to us. Silently we sat in the shelter listening to their story. Four of them were running together. The fourth one was Ruven, Feige's husband. They were being chased and shot at; Ruven was hit and dropped dead. The other three continued running. How did they know where to find us?

Apparently Ruven had told them about Góral's farm and that his wife and mother-in-law might be hiding there. At the news of Ruven's death, Gitel broke down in tears. Feige sat motionless, with a frozen look on her face. No doubt she did her crying in the darkness of the nights.

So this was how, for two years, fate threw together 11 people into a tiny shelter under a barn in northeast Poland. Together, we were to wage a desperate battle for survival.

The Górals

Góral's reward for hiding us was to be one half of the title to our Albinów farm. Additionally, while we were in hiding, he was given money and valuables which we had managed to bring with us. These valuables were given to him in installments, so as not to tempt him to spend the money too quickly and thus arouse his neighbors' suspicions. I remember one evening when Góral came down to our shelter and watched in silence as Father broke the hinges of a gold, jewel-studded cigarette case. Father gave Góral half of the case and kept the other half for another time.

The agreement between Father and Góral stipulated that Góral would get half of the Albinów farm only if all 11 of us were alive on the day of liberation. Obviously, Góral could have told us to leave and forcibly taken all of our possessions at any time. He did not do that. Why?

The Górals were devout, church-going Catholics. Was it their strong religious convictions? Perhaps, but religious devotion alone cannot fully explain their actions. Going to church every Sunday and kissing the hands of priests did not stop many Poles from murdering Jews.

The Górals were simple, decent folks. It is likely that their basic compassion and humanity did not allow them to turn us out. It is also probable that Jan Góral took the enormous risk of hiding Jews because of the irresistible lure of land. He had just a tiny farm, from which he eked out a meager living. The possibility of becoming the owner of much more land might have been a powerful incentive for him. Whatever his reasons, selfish or altruistic, I wish to do historic justice by paying tribute in these pages to this courageous man who saved our lives.[1]

---

1   Bill Tammeus and Rabbi Jacque Cukierkorn present 16 stories of rescue of Jews by Poles in their book, *They Were Just People* (University of Missouri Press, Columbia and London, 2009). When the number of rescues is compared to the total population, the conclusion must be that they were rare. Undoubtedly the fact that hiding Jews was punishable by death was a strong deterrent. Perhaps if more Poles felt that their collaborating neighbors would not have turned them in to the German authorities, more of them would have chanced hiding their Jewish neighbors.

The Góral family included Jan Góral and his wife, their married son Stanislaw (Stasiek for short), and his wife, Kasia, and three unmarried daughters. The three daughters only had one pair of stockings between them. Every Sunday they took turns wearing the stockings to church.

Stasiek was a sturdy, cheerful, pink-cheeked young man with a ready smile and a loud laugh (which he sometimes used to warn us of an approaching stranger). When threshing wheat with neighbors on the floor of our barn, he would raise his voice while telling jokes, in hope that we could hear them down in our shelter.

Mrs. Góral was a matronly peasant woman. I remember her mainly from the moments when she would emerge from the door of the farm house holding a pot of food and head in our direction. Before she left the house, one of the Górals would take a dog for a precautionary walk around the farm to sniff out any possible danger. We would eagerly watch her through the holes in the wall of the barn, for her arrival brought relief to our growling stomachs.

We stacked our dishes in a small niche in the straw in one of the walls of the shelter. The dishes were also used by the local mouse population for their own purpose – we had to shake out their droppings every time before putting food into them.

Our meals consisted primarily of mashed potatoes with rye bread, sometimes accompanied by boiled cabbage and soup. Once the food reached the shelter, Father did his best to divide it into eleven equal portions (no small feat, I presume). We squatted around him, watching. I recall a tense moment when someone accused Father of not being fair in apportioning the food. However, I don't remember any loud, sharp arguments taking place among us the entire time we were in hiding. Perhaps it was because we were afraid to raise our voices for fear of being heard outside. I am certain that human nature being what it is, and the continuous stress we lived under, there must have, at times, arisen tense situations. But we managed to keep our disagreements in check. We just could not afford to let internal arguments endanger us while the external world threatened us at any moment with annihilation.

The image of Jan Góral remains more clear to me than that of any other member of his family, probably because we got to see him more frequently. At that time he was probably in his late forties or early fifties. He had hollow cheeks and a thin, elongated face. I don't know the color of his hair, because I never saw him without a tall black cap on his head. I distinctly remember his watery blue eyes. They never seemed to be quite focused, probably because Góral was never quite sober. This was confirmed by the ever-present heavy odor of vodka on his breath. Needless to say, his drinking habits were a source of constant worry to us. We feared that some day, after imbibing heavily with his friends in town, he might blurt out something which would give us away. But, fortunately for us, Góral knew how to hold his liquor. His tongue never slipped. Sometimes he would come down to us in the shelter with a special treat – a bottle of home-brewed vodka (then popularly known as "bimber") and a dish of salted strips of raw bacon. He drank with relish, slowly raising the glass to his lips and then dumping the contents into his mouth with a swift backward toss of his head. This was invariably followed by a long "hooooooh" sound riding on a powerful wave of alcohol-laden air. He shared the bottle with us (even I was allowed to take a sip). In order to counter the incendiary effect of that powerful brew, we slowly chewed on the strips of raw bacon. At times Góral would doze off in the shelter. It may have been a convenient place for him to get away for a while from the hassle of daily farm chores.

The Barn

For the 11 of us sheltered underneath the barn, the structure became a place of refuge and hope. As far as we were concerned, there existed only two worlds: the world inside the barn, where life and hope lingered on, and the one outside, where certain death awaited us.

The refuge where we lived for nearly two years consisted of three major areas: the shelter underneath the barn, the passageway, and the main floor of the barn. The most important was the shelter, which was dug under the ground level of the barn and was camouflaged with bales of straw. This was where we ate and slept and to where we retreated at the slightest sign of danger.

The shelter was approximately six to eight meters (18 to 24 feet) long, two meters (six feet) wide, and one and a half meters (five feet) high. It had straw walls and a straw ceiling. Small saplings and branches formed beams which provided reinforcement and prevented the bales of straw piled on top from collapsing on us. The earthen, clay-like floor was covered with a wooden plank, where we placed straw and blankets to make it softer for us to sit and sleep. There was no room for anything other than the 11 of us; no table, chair or bed. We had to do everything in a sitting, or squatting position. Moving around inside the shelter was possible only in a bent position, and usually required stepping over someone. I was the only one small enough to stand upright. The one who suffered most was Mendel, the tallest in the group. He had to walk almost completely bent over.

Our only light was a kerosene lamp which hung on one of the wall-supporting wooden beams. Its proximity to the dry straw in the wall was a source of a constant, gnawing fear. We knew that if a fire broke out in the shelter, we would be in mortal danger. Either we would perish in the flames inside the barn, or be forced outside, there to face certain death. One evening this almost happened. The straw near the lamp caught fire, and flames began to race from one stalk to another. In unbelievable panic we threw everything we had – water, blankets, clothes – at the fire. Mercifully, the flames disappeared.

The air in the shelter was thick and unpleasant and must have been quite unhealthy. The only source of ventilation was the trap door in the ceiling near one of the corners of the shelter. The opening was square, about 60 by 60 centimeters (two by two feet). The air that came through the trap door came from inside the barn, and had its own distinctive smell.

The kerosene lamp undoubtedly did its part to degrade the air we breathed, but the main culprit must have been the ubiquitous straw that surrounded us. It was there all the time and everywhere, in the shelter and outside of it. The smell of straw will stay with me forever. The first time I visited a kibbutz in Israel, I came across bales of straw piled in the yard. As we walked by these bales, their smell instantly brought back the image of the shelter.

Dry straw has a rather pleasant smell, but wet straw emits a foul odor. For this reason we dreaded the coming of the rainy seasons. The plentiful rainfall of Polish autumns and the melting snow in the spring made the water level in our subterranean shelter rise. We watched helplessly as the water gradually rose and eventually flooded the wooden plank which served as our floor. We would then raise the plank a bit, only to see the next rain flood it again. The moisture and the smell of the rotting straw made our lives miserable. Whenever possible we took our clothes and blankets out of the shelter to dry in the passageway.

We spent more than 700 nights in the shelter, and each one was an exercise in discomfort and restlessness. To make room, we had to lie shoulder-to-shoulder. The air was stifling and thick with the bodily smell of 11 people, who had at their disposal only the minimal means of personal hygiene. The trap door was left open each night and that helped some, but certainly not much on hot summer nights.

What made our days, and even more so our nights, particularly miserable were the vermin, which persistently feasted on us. We had every imaginable kind of blood-sucking pest living with us. The most obnoxious were the lice, but not far behind were the fleas and the bedbugs. The moment darkness set in, these pests stormed us in force. Trying to fall asleep under their onslaught was nearly impossible. Throughout the nights, even while asleep, we continuously slapped at ourselves in a vain effort to kill bugs. The large bedbugs were the most disgusting. When crushed, they emitted a nauseating smell. As for the mice, darkness signaled the beginning of their freedom. We could hear them scurrying through the straw all night long.

Our bathroom was a bucket set up in the chicken coop on the opposite side of the barn. The bucket was emptied every evening outside the barn. To reach it meant leaving the safety of the shelter and entering the interior of the barn, and we could do this only when it was safe to do so. For toilet emergencies we had a small tin bucket in the shelter. Góral occasionally provided us with newspapers, which served as toilet paper. The paper was crude and thick and we crushed it in our hands to make it softer before using it.

The area in the chicken coop where the toilet bucket sat was also where we took our "baths". On bath occasions the Górals brought us a bucket of water which we poured into a large bowl. Mother dipped a small rag into the bowl and washed the upper parts of our bodies. We dried ourselves with one half of a towel, which Mother called the towel's "upper half". The same procedure was repeated for the lower parts of our bodies, which we dried with the "lower half" of that same towel. Of the three women in our shelter, Mother, Gitel and Feige, it was Mother who paid strictest attention to personal hygiene. Sometimes a washing bowl was set up in the shelter, and we were all asked to leave, to allow Mother to wash herself in privacy.

To leave the shelter we had to climb a short ladder, lift a trap door and enter a passageway, which led to the interior of the barn. The passageway was about 8 meters (24 feet) long, 80 centimeters (32 inches) wide, and 1.5 meters (5 feet) high, which meant that we had to bend while moving through it. Like the shelter, the passageway was built of straw, with its wall facing the courtyard. At its far end, at ground level, was a small, cutout door, about 50 centimeters (20 inches) high with a provision to be locked from the inside of the passageway. When open, the cutout door allowed us to crawl out onto the concrete floor of the barn.

The shelter was, undoubtedly, the least comfortable, but also the safest place for us to be. While there, with the trap door closed, we were, practically, isolated from the outside world. We could speak in normal tones, though never loudly, for fear that our voices might penetrate the bales of straw piled above us. When the trap door was open, the voices from the shelter could be heard, though faintly, in the passageway. While in the passageway we spoke only

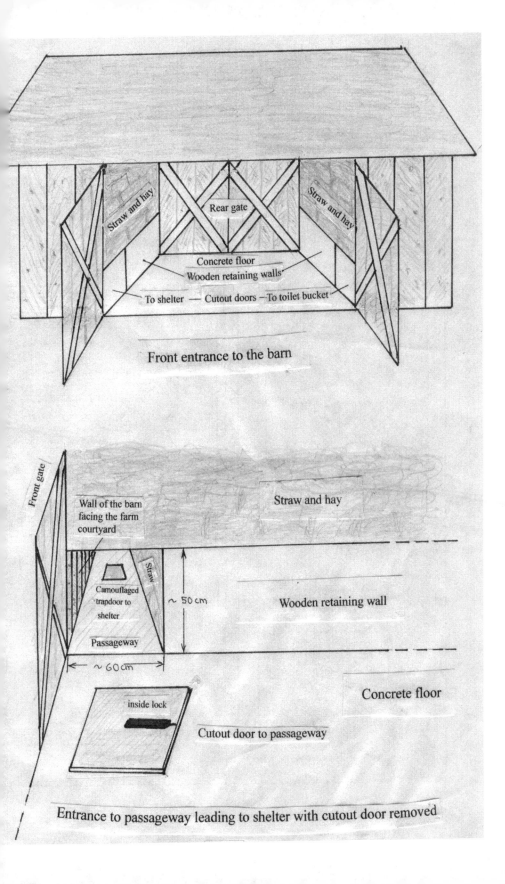

Straw and hay

Rear gate

Straw and hay

Concrete floor

Wooden retaining walls

To shelter — Cutout doors — To toilet bucket

Front entrance to the barn

Front gate

Wall of the barn facing the farm courtyard

Straw and hay

Straw

Camouflaged trapdoor to shelter

~ 50 cm

Wooden retaining wall

Passageway

~ 60 cm

Concrete floor

inside lock

Cutout door to passageway

Entrance to passageway leading to shelter with cutout door removed

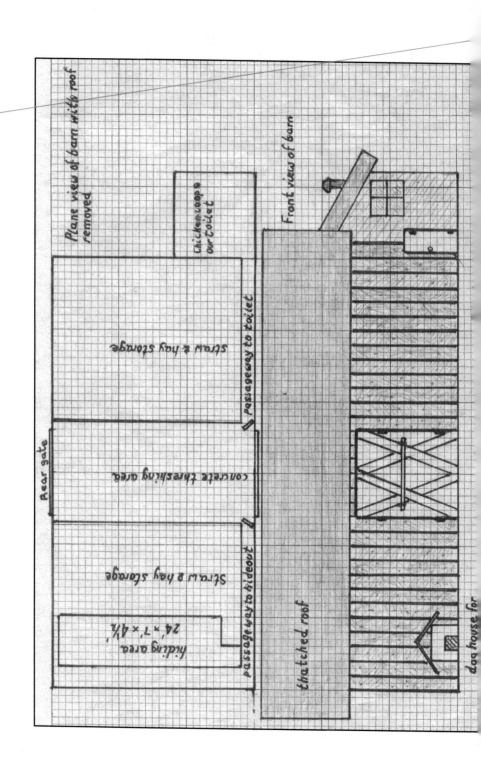

Plane view of barn with roof removed

Chicken coops or toilet

Straw & hay storage

Passageway to toilet

concrete threshing area

Rear gate

Straw & hay storage

passageway to hideout

hiding area.
24' × 7' × 4½'

Front view of barn

thatched roof

dog house for

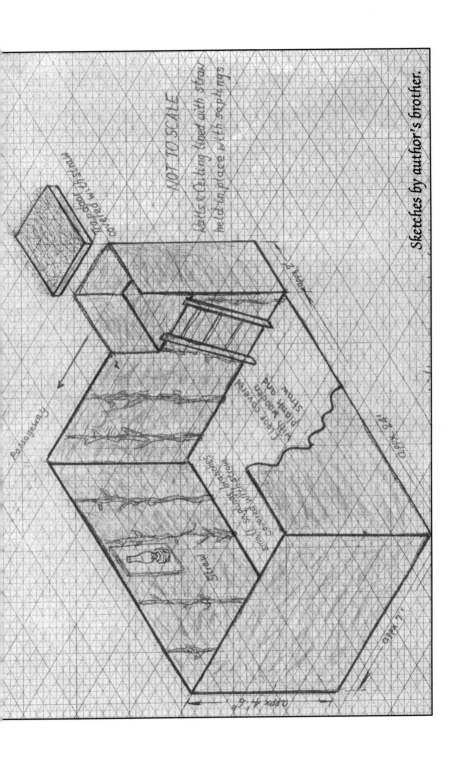

NOT TO SCALE

Slats nailing load with straw held in place with saplings.

Covered loop with straw

Passageway

Floor covering with wooden plank and straw

Covered spring branches covered with straw

Straw

Depth 4'6"

Approx 24'

Depth 24'

14' Wide

Sketches by author's brother.

in whispers, for fear that we might be heard in the interior of the barn or in the farm's courtyard.

The passageway gave us a chance to spend some time outside the stuffy confines of the shelter and breathe cleaner air. The knot holes in the wall of the passageway allowed us to peer at the courtyard of the farm. What we saw was the Górals' house facing us with the stable and cow shed on our right. We couldn't stand up in the passageway and, in order to look through the holes, we had to lie down. Anyone who came through the passageway had to climb over those lying there at the time (I remember holding my breath every time Gitel was stepping over me – an awful smell always emanated from under her skirt).

Through the holes in the opposite side of the barn, we could see the nearby forest and stretches of fields with some paths running through them. These views became monotonous. Nothing much was happening there, except for the Górals' routine farm chores. A welcome daily exception was the sight of Mrs. Góral stepping out of the house carrying a pot of food for us. Just outside the barn wall, near the entrance gate, stood a dog house. Its inhabitant was a scroungy, skin-and-bones creature, with patchy hair and the unpleasant habit of eating his own excrement. There were chickens running around in the yard. Occasionally, one of the Góral girls would step out to throw them grains while sounding high-pitched cries of "Cheep, cheep, cheep!"

Whenever possible, we made our way into the interior of the barn and spent as much time there as we could. The barn was divided in half by a concrete floor which at harvest time, was used for threshing wheat. On both sides of the concrete floor, behind a wooden partition, bales of straw and hay were stacked. In the partition, immediately to the left of the entrance gate, there was a thin vertical line. It was barely visible. This marked the location of the cutout door which led into our passageway.

The interior of the barn was the only place where we could walk fully erect and breathe air considerably cleaner than that in the shelter. It gave us an opportunity to relieve ourselves in the bucket in the chicken coop. We endlessly paced the concrete floor in an effort to preserve some degree of physical fitness. We tied two wide belts to the beams in the ceiling of the shelter and swung on them to exercise our upper bodies. We could stretch out and even hold whispered conversations while sitting on the bales of straw in the interior part of the barn.

Although the space inside the barn was the nicest place for us to be, it was also the most dangerous. When any of us were there, two people constantly peered through the holes in the walls to alert us to any approaching threat. At the slightest hint of danger, the lookout person snapped his fingers. This pre-arranged signal had an electrifying effect on us. It was an overriding command to stop all activity and quietly move in the direction of the cutout door. I remember the countless times when, my heart pounding, I tiptoed toward the opening – the distance to it seemed to decrease with maddening slowness. At any moment the gate of the barn might swing open and all would be lost. We dared not run. Silently, we tiptoed toward the cutout door, bent down, crawled into the passageway, and then climbed down the ladder into the shelter. The last person to enter the passageway locked the cutout door from the inside and lowered the camouflaged trapdoor at the shelter's entrance. The kerosene lamp was quickly extinguished. We sat in the shelter in complete darkness and in tomb-like silence.

Sometimes the warning was given because the lookout thought he saw a stranger approaching the barn. I remember how panic-stricken I used to get when, while sitting in the barn, I saw a sudden break in the beam of sunlight coming in through one of the holes. It could have been just a bird flying by. But it could also have been someone who, undetected, walked past the barn. Did he hear us? Does he suspect? Will he report us?

How did we spend our waking hours? What did we do with ourselves during the interminable weeks and months of our confinement? While in the passageway, all we could do was look through the holes in the wall of the barn at Góral's farmyard. But in the relative safety of the shelter we were able to pursue a variety of activities. We played cards. Someone in the group taught us a game called "501" and we played it endlessly. Jerry fashioned a chess board out of a piece of cardboard and molded chess pieces from bits of bread. He painted half of them red with beet juice, and the others he left in their natural color. Father taught us this wonderful, brain-stimulating game, and we played it often.

Occasionally Góral would bring us a Polish or a German newspaper. Father translated the German newspapers for us. We learned to read the news in the German-controlled press "between the lines". Thus the expression "Our victorious armies, for strategic reasons, shortened the front line", became, for us, synonymous with "retreat". We clipped maps out of the newspapers and together with the rumors brought from town by Góral, we were able to follow the progress of the Red army reasonably well.

Jerry clipped out political cartoons from the newspapers and amassed an impressive collection (he gave it to a Russian officer after liberation). The poisonous, vicious cartoons were primarily aimed against Jews and the allied armies. Many times, through their complaints about the allies' "barbaric behavior", the Germans inadvertently revealed their setbacks. For example, a cartoon showing a grinning, black American pilot trampling the Cologne cathedral, told us that German cities were being bombed. (We did not know at the time when we entered the shelter in October 1942 that Hitler's push into Russia was already beginning to slow. The Red army was gradually regaining the initiative in the battle for Stalingrad and the German forces were beginning to show signs of strain.)

Another daylight activity we pursued while sitting on the bundles of straw in the barn was cracking the lice in our clothing. I remember those little, white, multi-legged creatures sitting in the seams of my shirt. There was a red dot in the center of each louse – this was the blood they sucked from my body the night before. I placed the lice, one-by-one, between my thumb nails. Then I squeezed and listened to the popping sound with satisfaction. The agile, high-jumping flees were impossible to catch.

We had another, more aesthetic, activity. Mrs. Góral gave the women some wool and knitting needles. They would knit until the yarn was used up, and then they would loosen it and start all over again. It kept them busy. Mother noticed that I seemed to take interest in this activity and she taught me some basic knitting skills. I found this pastime enjoyable as it required manual dexterity and mental alertness. It also made time pass faster.

But our primary pastime was talking. We talked endlessly about everything and anything. We reminisced, worried and hoped. We spoke of those who had died, and of those whose fate was unknown to us. We spoke of the daily dangers facing us. We spoke of the lives we had led before the war, of the world which had gradually begun to seem unreal to us – a world in which we slept in beds, sat in chairs, ate at tables. But, above all, we dreamed – of the end of the war, of liberation, of being able to walk in the open, of not having to fear every shadow.

The Twelfth One

There were 11 of us in the barn. But, for a very short time, we became 12.

When Feige and Gitel arrived, we knew that Feige was married. What we did not know, then, was that she was pregnant. She managed to hide it from us for several months, but eventually, her condition became obvious. We realized that the day would come when an infant would be born in the shelter. What would happen then? A newborn baby cries. What would happen the next time our lives depended on our keeping absolute silence? When the slightest sound might result in our deaths? I could see the worry and tension in the faces of the grownups. I heard them whispering among themselves and with Góral.

On the day the baby was born, Jerry and I were told to leave the shelter and wait up in the barn. Before climbing the ladder I saw Father holding a pair of scissors over the smoky flame of the kerosene lamp (at the time I did not understand what he was doing, but obviously he was sterilizing the scissors to cut the umbilical cord). Jerry and I sat on the bales of straw above the shelter and waited.

Eventually we heard a thin, piercing cry from down below. A

baby girl was born. She was plump, healthy and full of life. She slept most of the time. Occasionally she would wake up and cry, and whenever that happened, Feige would frantically try to calm her. She fed and rocked her and sang softly to her. And while the baby cried, we sat benumbed with fear. Was anyone near the barn? Did anyone hear?

A few days after the baby was born, Mrs. Góral came down to the shelter carrying a pot of liquid. The following is forever engraved on my memory. I see Feige sitting on the floor, legs crossed, cradling the baby in her arms. Her pale face is bent over the small bundle of rags swaddling the baby. The pot of liquid sits by her side. She repeatedly dips a spoon into the pot and brings it to the baby's lips. The little girl eagerly swallows the liquid. She is happy and cheerful; she gurgles and blows bubbles. Her blue eyes stare up at Feige and her plump little legs kick the air. She falls asleep. Evening comes. I see Mendel, one of his hands resting on the ladder. Under his arm he is holding a small bundle, something wrapped in a rag. He lifts the cover at the entrance to the shelter and begins to climb. Something prompts me to look around.

Where is the baby? She is not in Feige's arms, she is not in Gitel's arms, she is not anywhere! I quickly turn my head in Mendel's direction but see only the lower part of his legs as he climbs the ladder and disappears into the darkness of the barn. We sit in silence. A short time later Mendel returns and... that small bundle is no longer under his arm!

O, Feige's baby! O, little girl! From the pages of this book, I ask your forgiveness! In the name of your mother and grandmother, and in the name of all of us who were then with you, I ask that you forgive us for what we did to you! We tried to save you. On the very same day you were born, the Górals' daughter-in-law gave birth to a baby boy. The Polish baby died at birth. We asked the Górals to take you in his place, but they could not do it. A local midwife had been present at that birth and knew that the infant had died. And so, a Polish baby, legally permitted to live, was born sick and died, while a Jewish baby, born healthy, had to be killed. The cruelty of fate sometimes exceeds all bounds.

O, Feige's baby! You may justly ask me, Who knows that I ever existed? Who will remember me? Of the 11 of you who were with me in the shelter, only you and your brother remain. And when you are no longer here, will not my memory vanish forever?

No, Feige's baby, not so anymore! From this moment on, not only my brother and I will know the story of your short life. Anyone who reads these lines will know that once there was a time when you breathed, slept and cried, when you were a warm, lovely little creature, when you were a living human being! I have planted your memory in their minds and they will carry it with them. They will recall what I told them about you, and they will tell others. In this way, your memory will live forever.

And so, dear reader, whenever you mourn the victims of the Holocaust, I ask that you think for a moment of that little girl whose bones lie somewhere near a barn in Poland, of that little girl who did not live long enough to be given a name.

Remember Feige's baby!

A Magic Moment Of Freedom

For two years, the world which existed outside was, for me, only a series of flat, one-dimensional images glimpsed through holes in the walls of a barn. But once, under the cover of darkness, Jerry and I were permitted to set foot outside. We were the only children in the group and we were to be given a taste of freedom, if only for a few moments.

The gate of the barn was opened. We bolted out into the night. I remember the exhilaration of running through open space, of hearing sounds all around me, of being engulfed by a breeze. We ran toward a small pond on the farm grounds and stopped at its edge. My heart beat fast; my eyes eagerly swept the surroundings. Looking behind me I could make out the contours of the farm house. On the still waters of the pond a clump of trees mapped itself against a moonlit sky.

I remember my sense of amazement at seeing a frog splashing

into the pond near me; I can still hear its croaking. The chirping of crickets filled the air. I breathed in deeply the myriad aromas of nature. There was magic all around me, and...there was fear... someone might see us!

Like two frightened deer we sprinted toward the barn, toward its protective life-saving walls. These few, magic moments of freedom will forever remain etched in my memory.

The Smell

A few months after going into hiding we began to sense a change in the air. A nauseating, putrid stench settled over the whole area. This acrid odor was constantly with us. It was all-pervasive, it seeped into every pore of our bodies, it permeated every fiber of our existence. We swallowed it with our food and drank it with our water. For a few weeks, awake or asleep, we drew it in with every breath. I do not know if any of us, even Góral, knew the source of this horrible smell.

It was only years later, after reading Holocaust literature[2] that I was able to correlate my memory of this smell with historical data.

In February 1943, as the fortunes of the German army on the eastern front began to decline, Himmler[3] visited Treblinka. By the time of his visit, Treblinka had been in operation for a few months. Already several hundred thousand Jews had been murdered in its gas chambers and buried in huge mass graves.

In an effort to erase all evidence of the carnage, Himmler ordered the bodies to be exhumed and burned. Accordingly, the operation (known by its code name, "Aktion 1005") was launched.

---

2   Steiner, Jean-Francois; *Treblinka*; Simon & Schuster Inc.; 1967. Sereny, Gitta, *Into That Darkness*, Random House; Pimlico; 1974. *Treblinka*, Muzeum Walki I Meczenstwa a Treblince; Oddzial Muzeum Okregowego w Siedlcach, 1988.

3   Himmler was the head of the SS, chief of the German Police, including the Gestapo (Secret State Police). He was responsible for the implementation of the Final Solution – the extermination of all Jews as ordered by Adolf Hitler.

March 2, 1943 – Smoke rises from the burning bodies in Treblinka. Photographed by Zygmund Zombecki. Received from Franciszek Donwecki who worked in the Treblinka train station. Presented at the 1965 Düsseldorf Treblinka trials. (With permission from the Yad Vashem archives.)

The half-decomposed bodies of the victims were hauled out of the mass graves and brought to specially-designed pyres, where they were burned.[4] The process took several weeks, and when it was over all the prisoners who took part in it were executed. The hideous activities then taking place in Treblinka, the macabre process of exhuming the bodies, the drinking parties of the Germans and the Ukrainians at night near the burning pyres, come as close to a description of Hell as one can imagine.

And so I learned the horrible truth. The smell we were smelling then was the smell of burning human flesh, the flesh of hundreds of thousands of Jewish people, the flesh of our families, of our friends. It was the smell of hell…!

The Ghoulish Act

After we went into hiding, I do not remember talking, or thinking, about the Zylberman family. I knew that they also had found a farmer who was willing to hide them. The last time I saw Mr. Zylberman was in the Kosów ghetto when he was discussing escape possibilities with my parents.

The friendship between the Zylbermans and my parents must have dated back to a number of years before the outbreak of the war. How else to explain the selfless invitation we received from them in the Warsaw Ghetto, which effectively said, "Come to us. Our home is your home"? They must have known that our presence would significantly affect their daily lives.

Now, as I look back at those years, I am convinced that the Zylbermans' invitation to join them in Kosów saved our lives. From reading about the rapidly deteriorating conditions in the Warsaw Ghetto in 1941 (which culminated in the massive deportations to Treblinka in mid-1942), I am certain that had we waited much longer, we would have found it impossible to escape. In the 18 months we lived with the Zylbermans in Kosów, we existed in a haven, a bubble, around which aktzyahs were taking place and tens

---

4   Even as Himmler's orders were being carried out, the killing at Treblinka continued at full pace. The only difference was that the bodies of the new victims were brought directly to the pyres.

of thousands of Jews were being sent to their deaths in Treblinka. The aktzyah in Kosów was probably the last in a chain of roundups which took place in the area.

The period of time we spent with the Zylbermans granted us a breathing spell. It allowed us to lead relatively normal lives for a while, and enabled us to find a place to hide. With this knowledge, I find the writing of this chapter, particularly painful.

Góral periodically came down to visit us in the shelter. Sometimes he came to drink vodka with us, and other times he came to share a rumor he had heard in town. Seeing him descend the ladder into our shelter always created in us a spike of worry – we feared that some day he might decide that he has had enough and order us to leave.

One day he appeared wearing a grave expression on his face. He told us he had met David Zylberman, who told him that the farmer who was hiding the family had turned them out. Knowing where we were, they headed for the Góral farm, in hopes that they could join us in hiding.

Góral refused. "I have trouble feeding the people I have. I can't take any more," he told him. He also refused Mr. Zylberman's plea to see Father.

I have only a faint recollection of that day in the shelter. The grownups and Góral spoke in whispers. After Góral left, we were in a state of shock and worry. We were sad and frustrated at not being able to help the family that had done so much for us. And, we wondered, if they were caught and tortured, might they give us away?

A few days later Góral showed up again. His face was grim. He told us that the Zylbermans had been murdered. Their bodies were found in the nearby forest. Mrs. Zylberman had been decapitated and her head had been taken away. Towards the end, Góral added that near the bodies of the Zylbermans also lay the body of a little white dog.

This news shattered us. It cast a gloom on our daily existence then, and left a pall that lingers to this day. This hideous act of cold-blooded murder has branded itself on my mind. On occasions, such as Holocaust memorials, I find myself recalling this tragic event and being buffeted by waves of emotion.

Should we feel guilty? Certainly not Jerry nor I. We were children then and had no say in the grownups' decisions. Should the grownups have felt guilty? Should they have tried to persuade Góral to grant the Zylbermans shelter? Perhaps they did, but I also can't help but wonder what our lives would have been like, and what would have been our chances of survival with another five people crammed into the shelter. The Zylberman episode is yet another confirmation that, in the Holocaust, at times, one person's death increased another person's chances to survive.

I try to think of what must have happened on that day when David Zylberman spoke with Góral, and how sad, desperate and frustrated he must have been to have to break the bad news to his family. He left his wife and children, Bumek and Mala, in the same forest where Mother and Jerry and I huddled in the cold winter night waiting for Father to return from Kosów. Our father returned bringing words of hope. We had a place to go, a place to hide. Bumek and Mala also waited for their father, hoping for similar news. But this was not to be.

When we were in the Warsaw Ghetto, the Zylbermans' life-saving message to us was: "Come to us; we'll find room for you." Regretfully, on that fateful day when they came to us seeking shelter, we were not able to reciprocate. This incident has left us with a deep psychological wound that will never heal.

Who killed the Zylbermans? I am convinced that the killers were local Poles for whom the Holocaust was an open, Jew-hunting season. At that time Polish gangs freely roamed the countryside, robbing and murdering Jews. One clue that it was not the Germans who murdered the Zylbermans was the decapitation of Mrs. Zylberman, and the fact that her head was missing. It is unlikely that the Germans would cut off the head of a Jew they killed and take it with them. To where, their army base?

This ghoulish act was undoubtedly committed by Poles, and the most likely reason was because Mrs. Zylberman's mouth was full of gold teeth, which the killers wanted to extract. They must have found it inconvenient to do this in the darkness of the forest, or maybe they did not have the necessary tools to do it at the time. Her head was cut off so that the killers could do their gruesome work at leisure in their nearby homes.

The little white dog who was found dead in the forest near the Zylbermans must have been no other than their beloved Zuch. This increases even further the mystery of Zuch's whereabouts during the family's ordeal. Just as I don't know where the Zylbermans and Zuch were during the aktzyah in Kosów, I also don't know where the dog could have been when they were in the shelter. Was he tied up outside? Somehow, he must have joined them on their trek to the forest after they were turned out by their farmer.

These questions will never be answered. But of one thing I am sure: at that terrible moment when one of the killers raised his weapon to strike the Zylbermans, surely Zuch jumped up and sank his teeth into the killer's arm. Zuch, the Brave, the little white dog with a Jewish heart, who ate only challah on the Sabbath, most certainly died in a desperate attempt to save his masters, our good friends, the Zylbermans.

Liberation

Most of the speculations as to when the war might end turned out to be naïve. When the war broke out, there were some who predicted that it would be short since England and France would immediately come to Poland's rescue. There were others who hoped that the Soviets would enter the war and, with the help of the western powers, quickly defeat the Germans.

All such hopes were summarily dashed by the Molotov-Ribbentrop pact of 1939 and the Germans' decisive victories in western Europe which followed. In 1941, the crushing defeat of the Soviets by the Germans in a "lightening speed" war, known as the "Blitzkrieg", appeared to hammer the last nail in the coffin of such hopes. The rumor we heard in hiding (probably in 1941) that the allies expected the war to last until 1946, was extremely disheartening to us. It seemed unlikely that we could continue to evade, for that long, the daily dangers facing us.

We knew that our salvation could come only from the defeat of the German army by the Soviets. We had no illusions that the armies of the western powers would be able to liberate us. After the battle of Stalingrad, the Soviet army began to push the Germans westward. The German retreat began. The tide of war was turning.

In the newspapers, which Góral occasionally brought to us, we began to see the names of cities in the Ukraine and Belarus, each one progressively closer to the Polish border. I remember the excitement when, for the first time, we came across the name of a Polish city. We realized that the Soviet army had penetrated into Polish territory.

Our hopes grew stronger by the day, but we knew that our lives were but tiny flames protected from a vicious storm by the thin walls of a barn. The slightest carelessness, a quirk, a whim of fate, and our lives could be snuffed out within minutes. We continued dreaming and hoping, as we perceived that the front line, the line of salvation, drew ever closer to us.

One day a curious incident occurred. I was in the passageway peering into the courtyard when I noticed, with great horror, a helmeted German soldier with a rifle slung over his shoulder walking toward the barn. Transfixed, I watched him heading straight in my direction. He sat down and leaned heavily against the wall of the barn. He was so close to me that, if it had not been for the wall, I could have touched him. Looking haggard and exhausted, he took off his helmet and wiped his face with a handkerchief. I dared not breathe. Others in the group had also spotted him, but there was no time to sound a warning. All anyone could do was stay frozen. After a short rest the soldier wearily rose and walked away.

This was a clear indication to us that the front line was not far away. We began to hear dull rumblings in the distance. We could not tell if this was the sound of a distant thunder storm or... perhaps... the roar of artillery? The rumblings ceased. An eerie quiet seemed to descend on the world around us. Unknown to us, in those very hours and minutes an invisible line, the line of fate was passing over us. O, how long had we waited for it to arrive! On one side of it, horror and death. On its other side, hope and life. Six million perished in the storm, six million candles of Jewish lives brutally blown out. Some continued to flicker, praying, hoping, to last another day, another hour to live until that line arrived.

And now it was here, slowly passing over the mass graves at nearby Treblinka, over the walking skeletons in concentration camps, over the dazed, exhausted human wrecks hiding in forests, attics and barns. The shadows of death were receding, the cries of agony were falling still.

Had the moment for which we had waited so long, finally arrived? Had we been spared? We remained skeptical and fearful.

Even when Jan Góral popped his head through the trap door and said, "They are gone! The Russians are in Kosów!", we still feared to make a move. We wanted to be sure that when we stepped out of the barn we would not fall prey to some retreating German unit or a roaming gang of local hooligans.[1]

We waited three days. When the moment to leave the barn finally arrived, we could not find the courage to leave through its main gate. Instead, a plank in one of its side walls was swung aside, providing a narrow opening to the outside. One by one we pushed our way through it.

The moment I left the barn will forever remain in my memory. I squeezed my way through the opening and unsteadily stepped outside. It was a mild, sunny day. The first thing I felt was a sense of unaccustomed brightness. I squinted and gradually opened my eyes. The world around me seemed to be exploding, expanding in every direction without limits. Instantly, the universe transformed itself from a flat, coin-sized image seen through a hole in a wall, into a giant, infinite cupola of immense beauty. There was distance and depth wherever I looked. My eyes traveled unhindered toward the sky – there were no walls, no roof to bar them! I looked down and marveled at seeing my feet pressing blades of green grass into the soft, yielding turf. Everything looked so different. The little bird who landed nearby and cocked his head at me looked so full and alive. Even the flies looked different.

I briefly glanced back at the barn. There were objects near it which for two years had been physically so close to me, yet I had never seen them because the walls of the barn had no holes pointing in their direction. I drew in deep breaths of fresh air, for the first time in two years, free of the smell of straw. I felt the warm sunshine on my skin and the soft breeze in my hair.

I heard Father urging us to start walking. I took a step; my head

---

1   I don't know the exact date of our liberation. I later found July 24, 1944 (Encyclopedia Judaica, Vol. 15, p. 1366) cited as "just prior to the entrance of the Soviet army into Treblinka." Since Góral's farm was so close to Treblinka, I assume that we were liberated soon afterward, most likely at the beginning of August 1944.

spun and I nearly fell (later I was told that I was then very thin and weak). I took another step, and then another and another, away from darkness, away from fear! I was nearly 12 years old. I left the dreadful past behind me and began my journey into the future.

After Liberation

We walked from Góral's farm to Kosów through open fields, carefully skirting inhabited areas. Yes, the Russians were in town, but they looked very different from those prisoners I had seen three years earlier being marched under escort through the streets of Kosów. What I now saw was a well-clothed and well-armed fighting force. Slung over the shoulder of every soldier was an automatic weapon called a "pepesha", with its characteristic round ammunition clip. These Russian soldiers were a boisterous bunch, given to dancing, drinking and singing (usually to the accompaniment of an accordion, a "garmoshka"). They were our liberators and we were grateful to them for saving our lives. But all too soon we discovered that many of them nurtured strong anti-Semitic feelings. We heard of one survivor who fell in gratitude at the feet of a Russian soldier, only to be roughly rebuffed and called a "dirty Jew".

We made our way to our former farm, Albinów, where we stayed for a short time. I use the word "former" since the Russians soon expropriated it and it was never to be ours again.

Albinów became the temporary gathering place for survivors from Kosów and neighboring villages. I recall only two of those survivors, a young man and woman, both probably in their twenties. He was dark with a sensitive face and a protruding Adam's apple. She was delicate with a thin, pretty face and large brown eyes. They were obviously very much in love. I don't recall their names, and I don't know anything about the young man. But I heard others tell the girl's story.

She had been brought to the edge of an execution pit with

hundreds of other victims. When the shooting began she threw herself into the pit and remained alive, buried under layers of dead bodies. The pit was left uncovered. After dark she made her way through the bodies, crawled out of the pit and ran into a forest, where she managed to survive.

There was a Russian army unit stationed in Albinów. We came in contact with some of the soldiers. They sat with us and drank their tea from portable water boilers, called "samovars" in Russian. Often, in order to make a samovar burn better, a soldier would take off one of his high boots to use it as an air pump with which to boost the flame (I had noticed then that the soldiers were not wearing socks but rather had their legs wrapped all the way to the knees with a bandage-like cloth called "oviyaki").

There were Jewish soldiers in this Russian army unit. Many still remembered some of the Yiddish language and took obvious pleasure in using it in our conversations. They listened with horror to the stories we told them. They were well aware of the killings of the Jews in the German-occupied Soviet territories, but had no idea of the extent of the mass murders which took place in Poland.

It was obvious that the soldiers lived in fear of the secret agents who prowled their ranks. They spoke Yiddish with us in low tones lest they be overheard. I recall one of them abruptly stopping in mid-sentence as he saw one of their officers approaching. He quietly whispered, "Eto nasha vlast" (this is our authority) meaning, of course, that the approaching officer was known to be an agent of the secret police.

Jerry described to a Jewish army captain what had taken place in the aktzyah in Kosów and how a local man by the name of Pietrzykowski had run wild in the streets killing Jews with an ax. The captain was so enraged that he took Jerry with him to Kosów with the intention of finding this man and shooting him on the spot. Despite several visits, they were unable to find him. Then the captain's unit moved westward and we moved to another town. Pietrzykowski probably lived out his years in peace and quiet without being the least bothered by the memories of his deeds.

One day Russian reporters came to Albinów. They interviewed us, the survivors. As we told our stories, they shook their heads in shock and horror. About a dozen of us (including one Treblinka survivor) were interviewed and our names were duly recorded. Some time later the story appeared in a newspaper, but only those of us having non-Jewish sounding names were quoted. There was no mention of the fact that the hundreds-of-thousands of Treblinka's victims were Jews – they were simply referred to as "Polish citizens".

From Albinów we moved to a larger, nearby town called Sokołów Podlaski, where we remained until the Russians liberated Pruszków, our hometown. In Sokołów, my parents opened a bakery (I still remember the delicious, crisp rolls) and, after studying for some time with a tutor, I began attending a public school. Thus, at the age of thirteen, my formal education had finally begun.

In Sokołów, as also later in Pruszków, I felt myself surrounded by an intense, although this time, covert anti-Semitism. It was everywhere – in every action and gesture of the Poles. Their eyes bespoke of an innate hostility and outright resentment at seeing us alive. Undoubtedly, in many cases this feeling stemmed from the fact that many Poles had unlawfully taken over Jewish property, and viewed every survivor as a potential claimant. But, I believe that this prejudice had much deeper roots. It was the result of having anti-Semitism instilled in them in their homes, schools and churches. For centuries they have imbibed it "with their mothers' milk". In fact, many a Polish mother would coax her child into eating by saying to him, "Jedz bo przyjdzie Żyd I cie wezmie" (eat or a Jew will come and take you). Generations of Poles grew up thinking of the Jew as an incarnation of the devil. This blind, irrational bigotry, has, in the Holocaust, turned many of them into merciless persecutors of their Jewish fellow-citizens.

Certainly, not all Poles behaved in this way. There were those who showed compassion and, despite the great risks involved, helped Jews. However, it is a sad, statistical fact that the rescuers were but a tiny minority – many more Jewish lives could have been saved had it not been for the willing collaboration of the

Poles with the Germans.[1]

Return To Pruszków, 1945

We returned to our hometown after it was liberated in January, 1945, four years after we were deported from there to the Warsaw Ghetto. The town had not been bombed and there was no visible damage to its infrastructure. The streets, the buildings, the stores, all looked the same as before. But the people in them were different. The familiar faces were gone and in their place were the faces of strangers. It was almost surreal. Out of the pre-war Pruszków Jewish population of some 3,000, only 30 remained alive. Mostly they were the only surviving members of their families. It was then that we realized just how fortunate we were and how unique was the way in which we survived– our immediate family of four had been able to stay together throughout the years of the Holocaust.

We moved into our old apartment at Kraszewkiego Street, number 12. Looking down from our balcony I could see the windows of the apartment where my maternal grandparents had lived across the street. Uncle Rywek had returned from Russia. He was deeply affected by the devastation of the town's Jewish community and the loss of his family. I remember seeing him look across the street at his parents' home and sob inconsolably on my mother's shoulder.

The anti-Semitism we encountered in Pruszków after the war was as unrelenting as it was before. Soon after our return I saw a Polish boy nicknamed Kotek on the street. He had grown considerably and was riding a bicycle. Overjoyed at seeing him, I stretched my hand out to him. He refused to accept it and disdainfully turned away from me.

---

1   Polish complicity took many forms – turning Jews over to the Germans, helping to hunt them down in the forests, uncovering and reporting their hiding places or outright murder. Not all Jews have Semitic features, and the Germans often found it difficult to identify them. In this they were frequently aided by Polish anti-Semites. All that was needed to seal a Jew's fate was to point at him and yell: "Żyd!" ("Jew" in Polish).

Another time I was cornered by three Polish youngsters who slapped and punched me. I can't forget the cruel, mocking cynicism in their eyes.

In an attempt to make friends and feel part of a group, I joined the Boy Scouts. The skits our group put on around the camp fires frequently made fun of Jews, portraying us as cowards and mimicking the Jewish accent. After one of these skits, a particularly disgusting one, the group leader came up to me and apologized.

I became aware of the pogrom in the Polish town of Kielce in July 1946, when some of the survivors arrived in our home in Pruszków (apparently, they personally knew my parents). I remember them walking through the door – heads bandaged, bodies bruised.

The pogrom was prompted by a blood-libel straight out of the Middle Ages. The Jews were accused of kidnapping a Polish boy for the purpose of ritual murder (actually, the boy had run away from home and had been hiding for a few days). In that outrage, 42 Jews (some of them survived the Holocaust in Poland and others returned from Russia) were murdered, in most brutal ways, by local Poles. Other anti-Jewish pogroms were taking place throughout Poland.

The exact number of Jewish victims murdered by Poles after the war between the years 1944 and 1947, is subject to debate, but is estimated at 1,000 to 2,000.[2]

We realized that, as Jews, there was no place for us in Poland. The chasm of hatred was too deep and too wide to bridge. Shortly after the Kielce pogrom, Father suffered a heart attack. When he recovered, we left Poland, I estimate in October 1946.

---

2   Dobroszycki, Dr. Lucjan, historian, 1973: "According to general estimates, 1,500 Jews lost their lives in Poland from liberation until the summer of 1947". Milyakova, Dr. Lidia, Russian Academy of Science, estimates the number at 1,500-1,800. Grajek, Stefan, historian: "Around 1,000 Jews were murdered in the first half of year 1946". Piotrowski, Tadeusz, historian, cites 1,500-2,000 between 1944 and 1947.

The Paths Of Our Lives

What happened after liberation to those of us who spent two years of our lives shoulder-to-shoulder in the barn?

The man named Berl was killed shortly after we regained our freedom. His love of liquor made him enter a pub in Kosów. There, intoxicated, he revealed to those around him where and how he had survived (ironically, this was exactly what we had feared Góral might do while we were in hiding). Shortly thereafter Berl was murdered, Góral was beaten, and the barn under which we survived was burned. Apparently the perpetrators, obviously local Poles, could not stomach the fact that some Jews had managed to survive.

The last we saw of the Rzepka brothers was in 1946, when we left Poland. They were then involved in the clandestine movement called "Aliyah Bet", the illegal immigration of Jews from Europe to Palestine. The Rzepka brothers helped us board a train to Czechoslovakia while posing as Greek slave laborers returning to Greece.

I heard that Gitel and Feige settled in France, and Feige remarried. I do not know what happened to the others who were in the barn with us.

For some time after liberation, even after we returned to Pruszków, we maintained contact with the Górals and assisted them financially. When we left Poland in 1946, all contact with them ceased. We were afraid that by corresponding with them we would expose them to persecution by their neighbors or by the Communist regime of Poland.

In 2007, Bill Tammeus and Rabbi Jaque Cukierkorn, authors of the book "They Were Just People", interviewed Jerry and devoted one of the book's chapters to the story of our survival. As part of their research they traveled to Poland to gather testimony from the rescuers or from their descendants. Despite extensive efforts, they were unable to find any trace of the Góral family. It is likely (and this is only speculation on my part) that after having been so cruelly treated by their neighbors, the Górals decided to relocate to some other part of Poland, perhaps even under an assumed name.

After leaving Poland, we spent five years in the western zone of Germany, first in the Displaced Persons camp of Feldafing and later in Munich, where Jerry and I studied electrical engineering at the Oskar von Miller Polytechnikum. In 1951, we emigrated to the United States under the sponsorship of the Jewish community of Davenport, Iowa. Eventually we relocated to Saint Louis, Missouri where Father died in 1980 and Mother in 1985.

I completed my engineering degrees in the State University of Iowa and at the University of Pennsylvania. I worked for RCA in Camden, New Jersey and McDonnell Aircraft in Saint Louis. In 1970 I was recruited by an Israeli engineering company and immigrated to Israel with my family.

Today I live in Tel-Aviv with Nomi, my Israeli-born wife, who is a piano teacher. I have two married children and six grandchildren, all of whom live near us. I taught electrical engineering at the School of Practical Engineering of Tel Aviv University until my retirement in 1998.

Jerry continues to live in Saint Louis with his wife, Linda.

We are both deeply involved in efforts to perpetuate the memory of the Holocaust.

Seeing Treblinka In 1944

One day, shortly after we were liberated, we set out to see Treblinka. I was 12 years old. We rode through pine forests in a horse-drawn buggy. Images from that visit to Treblinka, more than 65 years ago, remain with me to this day.

There was a large TREBLINKA sign at the train station, black letters on a white background. All that remained of the death camp was a huge, open space. The Germans had destroyed all the buildings and gas chambers and plowed over the earth. We saw scattered groups of local peasants digging in the ground, looking for gold teeth and coins in the ashes of the dead. We spoke little and in whispers.

The earth at the edges of the pits, where the scavengers were digging, was black. Father whispered that we were passing over the ashes of our people. Human remains were visible. Jerry saw a

Treblinka train station (Yad Vashem archives.)

The general view of the grounds of Treblinka in early spring, 1945.

charred hand lying in the dirt and wanted to pick it up, but Father refused to allow it. He did pick up a numbered metal identification tag of one of the victims from the Warsaw Ghetto.[3]

We entered a structure – I heard Mother whisper that maybe this was where the gassings were taking place. The exact nature of that structure remained a mystery to me for many years.[4]

Seeing Treblinka In 2000

In the year 2000 my wife, Nomi, her mother, Hela, and I went to Poland.

Our itinerary included a visit to Treblinka. I dreaded the prospect of seeing this horrible place again, but felt an irresistible force pulling me toward it. At the Jewish Historical Institute in Warsaw, I gathered additional information about Treblinka and Kosów Lacki. I found a map drawn in accordance with the testimony of survivors.[5]

The ride eastward evoked unpleasant memories. As we drove past farms, my eyes automatically searched out the barns. Names of towns which I had not heard since leaving Poland in 1946 flashed by the car windows. When I saw the sign giving the distance to the town of Małkynia, my heart began to pound. Małkynia is a major railway junction on the way from Warsaw to Bialystok. From here the death transports were directed to Treblinka. I remembered hearing the name Małkynia while we lived in Kosów with the Zylbermans; it was always mentioned in

---

3   This tag is now on display at the Holocaust Museum in Saint Louis, Missouri.

4   My research disclosed that the structure we had then entered was the house of a Ukrainian family (The Holocaust Chronicle; Publications International Ltd.; 2000; p. 517). The Germans had settled them there after destroying all of the camp's gas chambers and facilities and plowing over the grounds. The purpose was to make the place look like an ordinary farm – the Ukrainians planted crops and tilled the land, under which lie the ashes of hundreds of thousands of Jews...! The Red army forced the Ukrainians to move and burned the farm.

5   I had previously studied the model of the Treblinka camp in the Lohamey HaGetaot kibbutz in Israel.

In early spring 1945, local peasants scavenge for valuables in the ashes of the victims of the Treblinka death camp.

The house built at Treblinka after the camp had been demolished, in which a Ukrainian farmer was installed. Apparently this was the house we entered while in Treblinka in 1944.

some context with the dreaded word Treblinka. When the road sign to Kosów Lacki appeared, I climbed out of the car and stood staring at it for a while. Almost in disbelief, I realized that I was about to enter the town where, in 1942, we survived an aktzyah under the Zylbermans' warehouse, and from which we escaped to hide under a barn on Góral's farm.

A few minutes later I stood, overcome with emotion, in Kosów's main square. It was impossible for me to recognize anything from those years. The houses, the local peasants walking in and out of the stores, the young Pole who stood just a few feet away, uninterested in why I was using my video camera – all of them seemed to be saying, "The world did not care then and it does not care now".

We continued on. It was hard to believe that I was going to see Treblinka again. Riding in a car, rather than in a horse-drawn buggy as in 1944, we arrived within a short time.

Our first stop was the Treblinka train station. There, as I remembered, I again saw the sign TREBLINKA in big, black letters on a white background. The small station building now stands abandoned and ghost-like. The tracks on which the cattle cars of the death transports then stood are now rusty and overgrown with weeds. Here, the 60-car transports were split into three 20-car sections. The first 20 cars were pulled to the death camp four kilometers to the south, while the people jammed in the remaining 40 cars waited for their turn to die. When their cries annoyed the Ukrainian guards, they amused themselves by pumping shots into the wagons and watching blood seep out of the holes.

As I stood facing the tracks, I tried to visualize a string of 60 cattle cars stretching out into the horizon. I tried to imagine myself inside one such car, jammed in with people driven to madness by thirst and heat and the realization that soon we were all going to die. I could almost hear the clanking sound of the first 20 cars being uncoupled from the rest, the puffing locomotive beginning to slowly pull them toward the death camp. I could almost hear the laughter of the drunken, bestial Ukrainian guards and the sharp sound of the shots. I felt a sudden urge to quickly leave this accursed place.

Treblinka – Burial Pits

Some of the cranes used to transfer bodies from the burial pits to the pyres.
(From the Kurt Franz album.)

From the train station we continued to the death camp. Today a line of white stone slabs marks the perimeter of the camp where the three-meter high fence then stood. I stood on the unloading platform, where 2,000 people at a time were forced to disembark in a make-believe train station, complete with a false ticket window, a large clock (always showing the hour three) and flower beds. Had I been one of those disembarking, I would not have had much time to contemplate the scenery – a horde of Germans and Ukrainians would have rushed at us, shouting and indiscriminately beating us.

I crossed the line of the perimeter and walked into the former camp area. I was now in the Sorting Square. Had we been among the victims brought to Treblinka, it would have been here, in the Sorting Square, where Father would have been torn away from us. Here he would have been made to undress and, while being whipped, forced to carry his clothes to be sorted by special teams of prisoners.

I looked to the right and saw where the "Lazarette" (hospital) once stood. The elderly and sick were taken off the trains and sent there for immediate execution. Next to it there used to be a huge pit, into which the bodies of those who died on the way were dumped and burned.

I looked to the left where there is now a large wooded area. According to the map, there were no trees there in those days. Two barracks had stood there, one for women and children and the other for men. Mother, Jerry and I would have been chased into the one on the left; Father would have been driven, naked, from the Sorting Square into the one on the right. Once in the barracks, Jerry and I would have been forced to undress and, jammed in with hundreds of other naked, crying children, we would have waited until the women were ready. The door would then have opened and we would have been driven together with the women onto a path, cynically called by the Germans "Himmelstrasse" ("Street to Heaven"). The path was only two meters wide and as I ran I would have seen, out of the corners of my eyes, Germans with snarling dogs and Ukrainians armed with whips and bayonets. I

Railroad Tracks In Treblinka

1. Tracks branching to the left – to the ramp in Treblinka II where the victims were unloaded and herded into the Sorting Square.
2. Death train standing at the ramp.
3. Most likely the building housing the three old gas chambers. This photograph appears to have been taken before the addition of the building with the ten new gas chambers.
4. The guard tower near the pyres in the extermination area (compare with the Kibbutz Lohamey Ha-Gettaot model, page 120, and the Wiernik model, page 121).
5. Most likely the building that housed the Sonderkommando prisoners who worked in the extermination area.
6. Tracks branching to the right – to the Treblinka I penal camp.

would hear their shouts, curses and jeers. I would feel the sting of a lash across my back and I would run... run... run as fast I could with the mass of screaming, naked, frenzied people, all the time crying out for Mother. It is unlikely that I would have ever seen her or Jerry again.

The next thing I would have seen would have been a gate, which led into a low, sloped-roof building where the gas chambers stood. With my arms above my head, as I was ordered, I would be shoved with hundreds of others into one of the chambers. The pressure of the bodies around me would make all movement impossible. I would hear the metal door of the chamber close and the roar of the diesel engines come to life outside the building. And I would begin to die, slowly, in agony, gasping for breath. I would be crying as long as I could, but my voice would be drowned out by the screams of those around me. Twenty minutes later I would be dead and my body would be dumped into a pit. After the gas chambers were cleaned and the Himmelstrasse was sprinkled with fresh sand, the door of the men's barracks would open and Father, along with hundreds of other naked men, would be driven to his death.

With the aid of a compass and maps I brought along, I was able to fairly accurately locate the Himmelstrasse. It lay in what is now a grassy area between the trees where the barracks once stood and the place where the gas chambers were. The location of the Himmelstrasse is not marked. The average visitor to Treblinka will not know that this now-peaceful stretch of grass is the ground upon which hundreds of thousands of bare feet ran, carrying people to their deaths.

There are thousands of symbolic tombstones in Treblinka, one for each destroyed Jewish community. The tombstones were erected over the areas of the huge burial pits. In early 1943, Himmler visited Treblinka and ordered the bodies to be exhumed and burned. Those infernal pyres! Here is where that horrible stench we smelled in hiding came from. As I stood there, I recalled the survivors' testimonies, the hellish spectacle which took place here: huge excavators hauling out half-rotten bodies, heads and arms falling off, and those hellish pyres burning day and night… day and night. I shuddered… we were then so close, so close to all this![6]

In a daze I walked among the tombstones. Mercifully, there were no other visitors in Treblinka at that time – I was alone… alone in Treblinka! As I walked along, I read the names of the towns on the tombstones. There was the Warsaw tombstone, and near it the stone with the name of my hometown, Pruszków. Deeply moved, with head bowed and eyes closed, I paid homage to her victims.

Suddenly, my eyes fell on a tombstone with the name Kosów Lacki on it! I stood rooted to the spot, paralyzed, with blood pounding in my head. Here, after 58 years, staring me in the face was proof of what fate awaited me. The stone seemed to be saying to me: "You were supposed to come here with all the other Jews of Kosów Lacki! There was a place waiting for you in a gas chamber!" It was frightening, surreal. I felt like I was looking at my own grave.

At the foot of the monument marking the place where the 13 gas chambers stood, at the epicenter of evil, I stood benumbed. I was to die at this very spot! Here, in this abyss of hell, existed a horrible monster who, for years, had been searching for me… and he was then so close… so close to me…! I began to cry.

I took one, last look around, at the trees where the barracks once stood, now bending gently in the afternoon breeze, at the grass growing where the Himmelstrasse once was, at the tombstones erected over the ashes of hundreds of thousands of Jewish men, women and children. Treblinka looked so serene, so peaceful. It was so quiet in Treblinka… so very quiet. The only sound I heard were my own sobs.

---

6   One day, as I looked out through a hole in the wall of the barn, I saw a huge, billowing column of smoke rising on the horizon from the direction of Treblinka. Later we heard from Góral that at that time an uprising took place there. That column of smoke came from the fires which the escaping prisoners set to the camp's facilities. The fact that we could see it from our hiding makes me shudder at the realization of just how close we were to this hellish place.

Treblinka 1987

*(Visited by Michael Koenig
on September 2, 2000)*

The victims would be stood in a row – ready for the "chase" – naked and barefoot even in the worst winter days. The condemned ran between rows of torturers who shouted, battered them with their whips, pricked them with bayonets. Dogs tore chunks of flesh from the victims' bodies. The condemned screamed and cursed and howled with pain. Children cried. Women were frantic with fear. In order to increase capacity, the people were made to enter the gas chambers with their arms raised above their heads.

The shadow cast by the monument at the moment this picture was taken in 1987 is roughly where the "Himmelstrasse" was.

This is the area where the burnings took place. Here stood the pyres.

Symbolic pit.

Her(...) wher(...) gas ch(...) stood. south the 3 o(...) with a (...) of 100 each. (...) north w(...) 10 new(...) with a c(...) of 200 each.

Now Grassy Area

"HIMMELSTRASSE" ("DER SCHLAUCH")

Approximately 2 m (6 ft) wide and 150 m (450 ft) long

Women and children went first.

The men followed.

Now Wooded Area

#17 ON MAP

#18 ON MAP

Now Wooded Area

Womens' and Childrens' Barrack

Here the women and children were made to undress. The womens' heads were shaven and intimate parts of their bodies were searched for hidden valuables.

Mens' Barrack

Men had to undress already in the Sorting Square. They were packed in here naked, waiting until the women and children died.

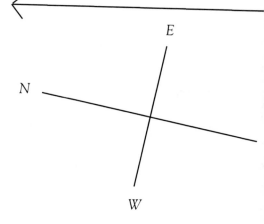

To The Barracks

N

E

W

Muzeum Walki i Męczeństwa w Treblince
Oddział Muzeum Okręgowego w Siedlcach

The area of Treblinka II was roughly 400 x 400 meters. The tombstones have been erected where the burial pits were. Here, underneath one's feet lie the ashes of 850,000 Jewish men, women and children.

Approximately here is the Kosów Lacki tombstone.

One of these is the Pruszków tombstone.

Warsaw tombstone.

To the "Lazarette" (The "Hospital") where the sick and elderly were sent for immediate execution.

The "Sorting Square"

Here families were broken up without being allowed the opportunity for farewells. Men were immediately separated from women and children and were made to undress. While their heads and faces were being whipped, they had to snatch armfuls of clothing and bring them to a large pile to be sorted.

From Unloading Platform (The "ramp")

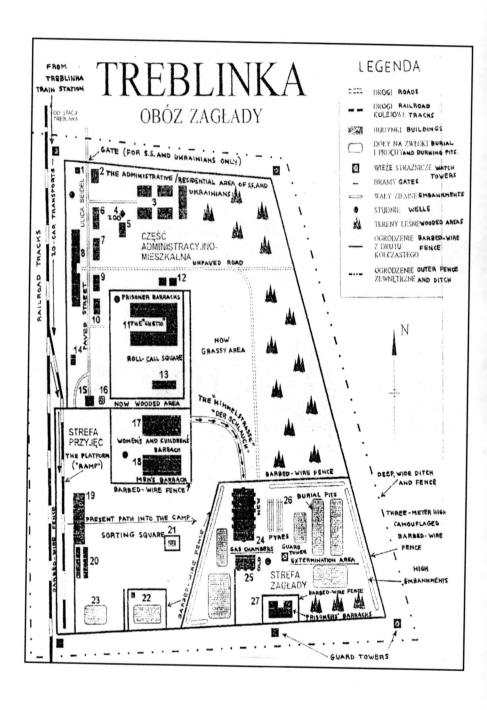

TREBLINKA

OBÓZ ZAGŁADY

LEGENDA

Treblinka Diagram Legend

1. Guard Tower
2. The kommandant's residence and office
3. Barracks of the Ukrainian guards
4. Zoo
5. Barracks where valuables were sorted
6. Doctors' and dentists' offices and barber shop for the SS-men
7. Service barracks
8. Residential quarters of the SS-men
9. Warehouse for storing textiles
10. Bakery
11. Prisoners' barracks (also known as "The Ghetto")
12. Stables and pigpens
13. Prisoners' latrine
14. Gas station
15. Garage
16. Coal storage
17. Barracks in which women and children had to undress. Here the women had their heads shaved and intimate parts of their bodies searched for hidden valuables.
18. Barracks into which naked men were herded. Here they waited until the women and children were gassed and, like they, were driven through the "Himmelstrasse" to the gas chambers. The "Himmelstrasse" (also called "Der Schlauch") was the 2-meter wide, about 150-meter long, curving path along which the victims were chased to the gas chambers.
19. Warehouse for the sorted belongings of the victims. Its front (facing the unloading platform) was made into a make-believe train station to delude the victims.
20. Additional warehouse
21. Latrine
22. "Lazarette" (the "Hospital") to which the sick and elderly were sent for immediate execution. They were made to sit on a bench facing a huge pit and were shot in the neck. Their bodies tumbled into the pit where they were burned.
23. Burial pit into which the bodies of those who died on the way were dumped and burned.
24. The 10 new gas chambers with a capacity of 200 people each.
25. The 3 old gas chambers with a capacity of 100 people each.
26. Pyres where the exhumed bodies were burned.
27. Barracks for prisoners who worked in the extermination area.

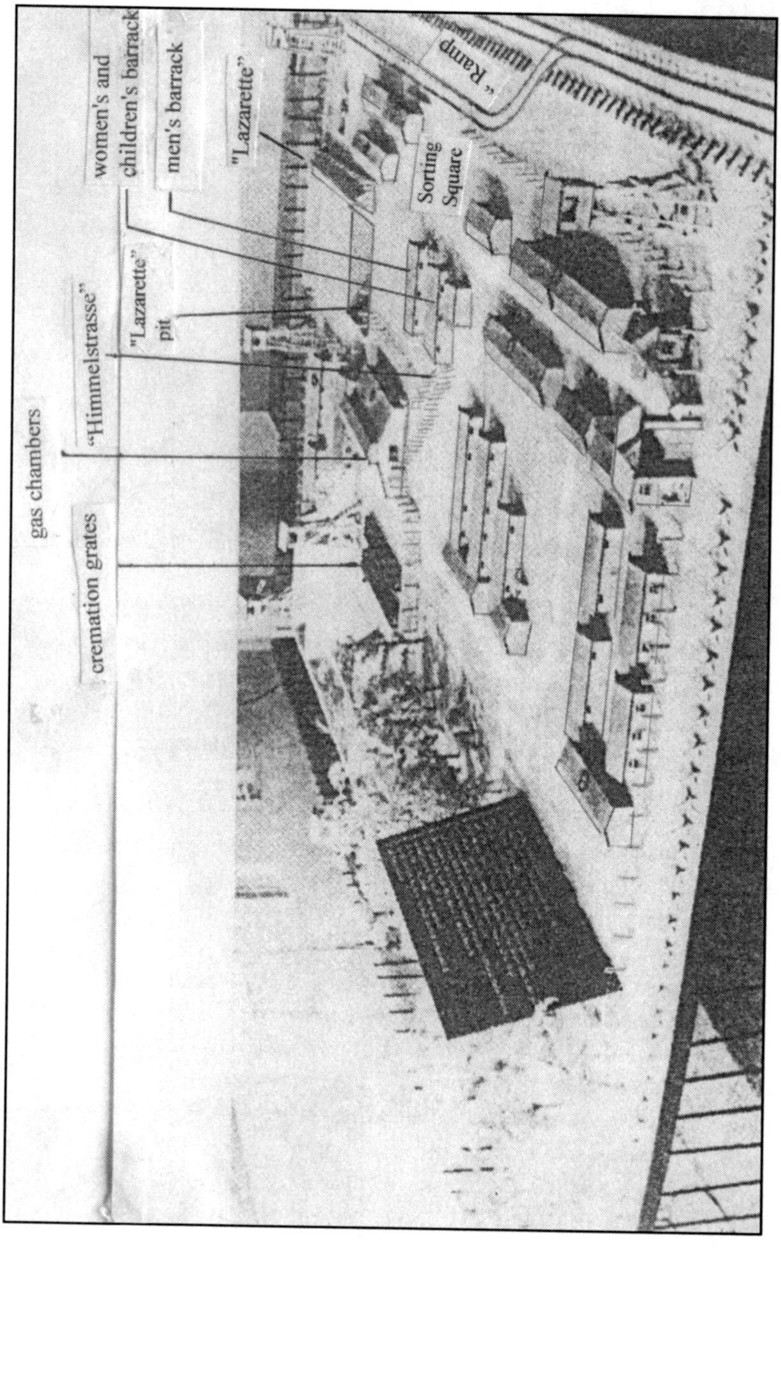

Model of Treblinka death camp at the Holocaust museum, Kibbutz Lohamei Ha-Gettaot.

gas chambers

"Himmelstrasse"

cremation grates

women's and children's barrack

men's barrack

"Lazarette"

"Lazarette" pit

Sorting Square

"Ramp"

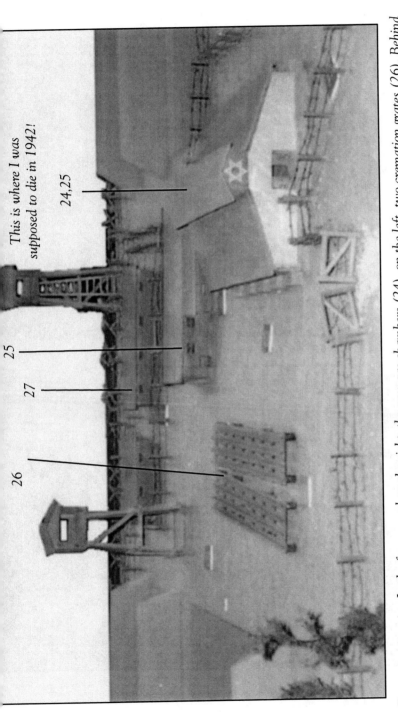

This is where I was supposed to die in 1942!

24,25

25

27

26

Extermination site: In the foreground on the right, the new gas chambers (24), on the left, two cremation grates (26). Behind the new gas chambers the smaller building of the old gas chambers is visible (25). In the background the two Sonderkommando barracks (27). The Wiernik model: http://www.deathcamps.org/treblinka/wiernik.html (Wiernik is a Treblinka survivor.)

These tombstones in Treblinka were photographed by my grandson Alon Lubinski in 2011. The tombstone of Pruszków commemorates my hometown. The one of Kosów Lacki commemorates the town where I survived an aktzyah and from which I was to be taken to be murdered in Treblinka.

The Treblinka Memorial Monument – erected in 1964 at the site where the gas chambers stood.

REGISTER
OF
JEWISH
SURVIVORS

II

LIST OF JEWS IN POLAND

4358 /

(58.000 NAMES)

JERUSALEM 1945

PUBLISHED BY THE JEWISH AGENCY FOR PALESTINE / SEARCH BUREAU
FOR MISSING RELATIVES

anowicz Łaja, Zamość
anowicz Natan, Zamość
anowicz Srula, Zamość
er Beniamin, Warszawa
er Olga, Rychbach
er Wilma, Peterswaldau
er Dr. Zygmunt, Kraków
en Zygmunt, Lwów
n Szrajerman Szejna, Łódź
r Adolf, Łódź
r Anna, Warszawa
r Jadwiga, Łódź
ltine Zalman, Warszawa
lhner Zelman, Lublin
enow Diwaja, Berg.-Belsen
ińska Bela, Berg.-Belsen
ińska Ewa, Kielce
ińska Ina, Łódź
ińska Janina, Częstochowa
iński Izak, Łódź
iński Jan, Zamość
iński Mordka, Koło
iński Szlama, Łódź
iński Szymon, Konin
ler Dago, Lwów
ler Dora, Kraków
ler Erna, Warszawa
ler Franka, Kraków
ler Fryda, Kraków
ler Ita, Kraków
ler Jakub, Bochnia
ler Pola, Tarnów
ler Rema, Kraków
ler Rozalia, Matthausen
ler Syma, Kraków
ler Zofia, Kraków
ler Zuzanna, Kraków
ner Alter, Zawiercie
ner Alter, Peterswaldau
ner Eleonora, Bydgoszcz
ner Fajwel, Częstochowa
ner Heniek, Sosnowiec
ner Jan, Kalisz
ner Pesa, Warszawa
ner vel Kępińska Regina, Łódź
ner Witka, Lublin
Estera, Warszawa
Maria, Warszawa
Simi, Bydgoszcz
r Albert, Tarnów
r Albin, Kraków
r Anita, Nowy Sącz
Hinda, Peterswaldau
Hinda, Sosnowiec
r Regina, Kraków
r Sabina, Kraków
Adam, Nowy Sącz
Anna, Kraków
Baszewa, Bydgoszcz
Bebi, Rychbach
Berta, Warszawa
Bobi, Peterswaldau
Chaja, Kraków
Chana, Matthausen

Koenig Ella, Rychbach
Koenig Georg, Oświęcim
Koenig Chuna, Linz
Koenig Jakub, Kraków
Kienig Mania, Bergen-Belsen
Koenig Milos, Oświęcim
Kenig Minia, Warszawa
Kenig Rachela, Będzin
Koenig Rafael, Matthausen
Keniger Józef, Katowice
Koenigit Leontyna, Warszawa
Kenigsberg Balbina, Częstochowa
Kóenigsberg Barbara, Kraków
Keniksberg Cecylia, Warszawa
Koenigsberg Celina, Kraków
Koenigsberg Chaim, Rychbach
Kenigsberg Eliasz, Łódź
Koenigsberg Ita, Warszawa
Kenigsberg Erlichman Ita, Łódź
Koenigsberg Janina, Warszawa
Koenigsberg Josef, Rychbach
Kenigsberg Lena, Łódź
Koenigsberg Lenka, Warszawa
Koenigsberg Lońka, Warszawa
Koenigsberg Maks, Lwów
Kenigsberg Maria, Kraków
Koenigsberg Marian, Kraków
Kenigsberg Mery, Warszawa
Kenigsberg Mojżesz, Częstochowa
Koenigsberg Roman, Kraków
Kenigsberg Rosa, Rychbach
Koenigsberg Sabina, Kraków
Kenigsberg Władysław, Kraków
Kenigsberg Zygmunt, Łódź
Koenigsberger Tauba, Sosnowiec
Koenigstein Alina, Warszawa
Koenigstein Elżbieta, Warszawa
Kenigstein Estera, Będzin
Kenigstein Fajga, Warszawa
Koenigstein Genia, Łódź
Koenigstein Janina, Łódź
Kenigstein Ignacy, Łódź
Kenigsztejn Izydor, Kosów
Kenigstein Jadwiga, Warszawa
Kenigsztejn Jerzy, Kosów
Kenigsztejn Mania, Kosów
Kenigstein Marek Dr., Warszawa
Koenigstein Marian, Łódź
Kenigsztejn Michał, Kosów
Koenigstein Mordka, Sosnowiec
Koenigstein Mordka, Chęciny
Kenigsztajn Mordka, Łódź
Koenigstein Piotr, Warszawa
Koenigstein Romana, Warszawa
Koenigstein Roza, Rychbach
Koenigstejn Rosa, Będzin
Kenigsztajn Rózia, Łódź
Koenigstein Stefan, Warszawa
Kenigsztajn Szaja, Łódź
Kenigsztajn Szyja, Piotrków
Kenigstein Zysze, Łódź
Kenigswejn Regina, Warszawa
Kenigswejn Sara, Warszawa
Kenigswejn Szmul Zanwel, Warszawa

Keppel Roma, Lwów
Kepler Julia, Kraków
Kepner Nuna, Lwów
Kerbel Dawid, Ostrowiec
Kerbel Maita, Kraków
Koerbel Manja, Kraków
Kaerbel Maria, Oświęcim
Koerbel Moryc, Kraków
Kaerbel Maurycy, Oświęcim
Kaerbel Rozalia, Oświęcim
Kerbel Sara, Ostrowiec
Kerber Abram, Sosnowiec
Kerber Abram, Warszawa
Koerber Bina, Kraków
Kerber Hanna Lora, Gliwice
Kerber Ida, Gliwice
Kerber Lipe, Linz
Kerc Franciszka, Warszawa
Kerczenblat Frania, Peterswaldau
Kerman Rózia, Bergen-Belsen
Kern Beniamin, Przemyśl
Kern Bina, Kraków
Kern Emil, Katowice
Kern Icek, Sosnowiec
Kern Mojżesz, Przemyśl
Kern Moses, Kraków
Koerner Abraham, Rzeszów
Kerner Bersie, Warszawa
Kerner Cela, Łódź
Kerner Felicja, Bergen-Belsen
Kerner Gizela, Warszawa
Koerner Helena, Warszawa
Kerner Henryk Dr. Warszawa
Kerner Jadwiga, Warszawa
Kerner Lipa Dr., Warszawa
Kerner Lipa, Lwów
Kerner Maks, Biała Podl.
Kerner Mania, Kraków
Kerner Mirosław, Lwów
Kerner Rita, Bergen-Belsen
Kerner Jaryczowa Roza, Kraków
Koerner Róża, Lublin
Koerner Ryszard, Lublin
Kernkraut Samuel, Kraków
Kersten Adam, Łódź
Kersz Sala, Bergen-Belsen
Kerszbaum Fiszel, Łódź
Kerszbaum Rózia, Łódź
Kerszberg Pola, Łódź
Kerszenbaum Dobka, Sosnowiec
Kerszenbaum Edka, Warszawa
Kerszenbaum Pola, Częstochowa
Kerszenbaum Rafał, Łódź
Kerszenbaum Szajndla, Międzyrzec
Kerszenblat Franka, Sosnowiec
Kerszenhorn Hersz, Hrubieszów
Kerszenzon Josef, Chełm
Kerszner Freda, Suchedniów
Kerszner Genendla, Suchedniów
Kerszner Genendla, Suchedniów
Kertiss Gisi, Rychbach
Kerzner Romana, Warszawa
Karzner Rysia, Kraków
Kaess Irena, Warszawa

Kenigsztein, Michal (the author)

Part Two
The Holocaust In My Poetry

The Abyss

The abyss...
where all reason and life
ceased to exist,
from which the tentacles
of a horrible demon
sucked in thousands
into its innards,
from which the stench
of burning bodies
permeated the air we breathed,
as we clung to the edge ...
of Treblinka's abyss.

O, Were All This But A Bad Dream!

I had a monster chase me for years,
with millions of others I ran in great fear;
I heard their cries – I felt my own tears
stream down my face when death seemed so near.

I saw many around me miss their stride,
stumble and falter, fall to the side –
men, women and children with no place to hide,
with no hope left, no strength to spare,
defeated, exhausted, filled with despair.

There are times when I wish that I could pretend
that things never happened – that they never took place,
that the millions who vanished without leaving a trace
are still out there, alive… as they were in those days.

There are times when I wish I could make it all seem
just an innocent nightmare… just a little bad dream!

The Barn[1]

Hidden from view, we vanished from earth;
although alive, the world thinks us dead.

If they will find us, our lives will be worth
less than a worm's which one grinds in the dust
less than a bird's in the jaws of a beast...

Through the holes in the boards, with pencils of gold,
the sun traces figures, circles and lines,
on the concrete floor and the bundles of straw
in the gloomy twilight of the barn's confines.

Through the holes I gaze – they're my eyes on the world;
I sit glued to them for hours on end...
through them I see nature, distance and depth,
fields, trees and grass and small, narrow paths
leading away into somewhere...

From where do paths come, where do they go?
Will I be ever allowed to know?

Will my eyes be ever again allowed
to fly unhindered towards the sky?

Will I ever again know the joy of being engulfed by space?
Will I be ever allowed again to feel upon my face
the caress of the sun, the wind, the rain...?

Or will they some day lead us outside...

Will I cling to my dear ones sobbing and crying?
Will I hear the shots... will I feel the pain?
What is it like to be dying?

---

1   1942-1944.

If Only You Could Have Promised!
(Feige's Baby)

O little girl, O little baby,
you were born so healthy but had to die...

If only you could have promised to be quiet,
if only you could have promised not to cry!

Your mother bore you during the war,
under a barn – in a shelter of straw,
and if you were not quiet,
eleven people would die...

that's why, little baby,
we could not let you cry!

I remember the flame of the kerosene lamp
singeing the scissors for cutting your cord;

I remember so clearly your first, lusty yell
forcing its way through the shelter's trapdoor.

Above, in the farmhouse, at the same time,
a baby like you was born and died.

We wanted to put you in the dead baby's crib,
but the midwife knew...

that's why, little girl,
you had to die too...!

I remember your mother holding you tight
while placing a spoon to your lips...

"Sip your tea, baby…hush and don't cry,
you'll soon hear eternity's sad lullaby!"

I am sorry, O baby, that you had to die…

If only you could have promised to be quiet!
If only you could have promised not to cry!

The Fourth One
(To Ruven, the man who ran to see his child)

They say that,
as the Jewish infant lay amidst straw,
there was rejoicing on earth –
a bright star shone and three men set out
for the humble place of its birth.

Centuries later, under a barn,
surrounded by fear and death,
another Jewish infant was born...

No star appeared in the skies,
no heavenly trumpets were heard,
when, dodging bullets, four men set out
for the humble place of its birth.

Away from the camp of Treblinka,
through sands and woods of pine,
four men ran towards the barn
but... only three arrived!

The fourth one, who died, ran to his child
whom he has never seen before,
one-thousand-nine-hundred and forty-three years
after the birth of the lord.

Zuch[1]

He was little, white, with pointed ears,
a pet of the family with whom we lived.

He was gentle and kind…

A Jew at heart was this little fellow –
from sunset on Fridays until Sabbath's end
he refused to eat bread and ate only "challah"

One day, as I played with the family's son,
while Zuch sat near us looking idly on,
the boy slyly said, "Point a finger at me!"

Some new game, I thought, and did as he asked.

A metamorphosis took place in the dog…
eyes flashing with fury, teeth bared in a snarl,
he was, obviously, ready to jump at my throat…

I hastily lowered my arm…

"He saw soldiers shoot puppies", the boy calmly explained,
"since then he protects me –
he thought that your finger was a gun in your hand".

Our ways parted…

The boy and his sister with their parents
were found in a forest… butchered… beheaded…

At their side lay the little, white dog
who refused to eat bread on the Sabbath…

---

1   Zuch was the dog of the Zylberman family in whose home we
lived in 1941 in the town of Kosów Lacki.

The Rocks[1]

Herr Kommandant was a good father…

He would hoist his son into the saddle
and gallop, trot and prance around –
his horse's hoofs recklessly kicking
at the round rocks on the camp's grounds.

But strangely, these rocks
had mouths and eyes,
produced dull sounds
when struck…

With his son in the saddle
he liked to gallop
among the screaming rocks…

---

1   As told by the escapees from Treblinka.

The Hammer[1]

The Ukrainian guard
was nicknamed The Hammer –

Start digging Jew, that's deep enough!
The Hammer laughs, the hammer hits…

Climb out now, Jew – for if you do,
I'll let you live!
The hammer hits…

Climb out, you Jew,
this one more time,
for if you do,
I'll spare your life!
The hammer hits…

This time I promise – I promise for sure!
The Hammer laughs, the hammer hits
the head, the chest, the legs, the arms…

I promise! I promise!
Just one more time! Just one more time!
So climb, you Jew,
climb for your life!

You are almost out of the pit, O Jew…
You are almost at the top…!

The hammer hits…
the hammer clicks…
time in the pit
comes to a stop!

---

1   As told by the escapees from Treblinka.

The Fleeing German[1]

We hear the sound of cannons
destroying the savage hordes.

A fleeing German soldier
approaches the barn,
leans against its boards.

I glare at him from behind the planks,
Go to the front line, you murderous villain!

Do you find it harder to fight Russian tanks
than killing unarmed civilians?

---

1   1944

It Could Have Been I...![1]

So pitiful, small, a cap on his head,
hands raised in surrender,
eyes frightened and sad.

When I gaze at his features
I am startled, amazed,
for I seem to be looking
at myself in those days...

We were almost the same age,
we resembled each other –
he could almost have been
my cousin or brother.

We lived in the shadow
of the wall of despair –
we watched the same sunrise,
breathed the same air.

It could have been I
in this picture instead,
with hands in surrender
held over my head...

But I am alive...
He's long since been dead!

---

1   A photograph of a boy at the liquidation of the Warsaw Ghetto.

What Was He Thinking...?

What was he thinking,
what went on in his mind,
when he aimed his weapon
at a fleeing woman,
when he squeezed the trigger
at a crying child?

What was he thinking,
what went on in his mind,
as he tore an infant
from his mother's arms?

Did not that youngster
whom he shot in cold blood
remind him of his son?

While forcing a man
to hang his father,
did he not think of his own?

While killing a woman,
did his thoughts never turn
to his sister, mother or wife?

While taking the life of an innocent child...

What was he thinking?

What went on in his mind?

O Tree In Treblinka![1]

O Tree in Treblinka, do you know
that where you sank your roots
a barrack once stood?

Do you know
that a naked child with fear in his eyes
stood in the space which your trunk occupies?

As I stared at you on Treblinka's grounds,
I saw that naked child,
I heard his frantic cries.

Then his image faded and disappeared,
but in his place another child appeared...
and then I saw another naked child
appear in his place...
and then... at a furious pace...
I saw another one... and another one...
naked, frightened, crying for mother
they appeared and were gone –
one after another... one after another...!

O Tree in Treblinka, do you know
that thousands of children stood in the space
you now occupy?
That where you stand... from this very place
these Jewish children
were sent to die?

---

1   In the year 2000.

It Is So Quiet In Treblinka Now![1]

It is so quiet in Treblinka now,
but in those days
dampened by sand embankments,
muted by camouflaged fences,
a hellish din must have filled this place.

The shrill whistle of the steam locomotives,
the grinding to a halt of the cattle cars,
the screech of the brakes, the screams, the curses,
the jeers, the barking dogs, the shouts,
the swishing sound of whips hitting faces,
the cries of the families being torn apart,
the roar of diesel engines at the gas chambers,
the crackling of shots, the shouts of despair,
the grinding and clanking of huge excavators
hauling the bodies out of mass graves...

It is so quiet now in Treblinka –
there silence reigns and nothing stirs –
now one hears only the chirping of birds,
now one hears only the rustling of trees...

Only the sobs of those who visit
disturb Treblinka's eternal peace.

---

1   In the year 2000.

How Can I Write…?[1]

How can I explain how I felt
while waiting for a train
to take me to Dachau… for a visit!

How many went there to never come back?
So how can anyone just "visit" Dachau?

Or how I felt at the journey's end
when the train stopped at the black-lettered sign;
a city named Dachau! Where people live now and lived then.

But how can anyone say "I live in Dachau."?

How can I write of the sadness I sensed
as I walked through the gate,
by the sinister towers, through the barbed wire fence?

How can I describe the terrible weight
crushing my heart like a stone –
the disbelief, anger, outrage,
the sudden urge to stand alone
on Dachau's hallowed, tortured ground
with my eyes tightly closed, my head humbly bent
without seeing a thing, without hearing a sound?

The museum – so cold, efficient and clean;
Now, hurry – the film is about to begin!

How can I describe the anguish I felt
as I sat in the dark with the light from the screen
searing my heart with the horrors of Dachau?

---

1   Dachau, 1976.

How can I write what I felt on the street
where the barracks once stood –
the road trodden daily by thousands of feet
of half-human slaves in striped prison garb,
driven and beaten by murderous guards?

So how can I explain, how can I describe...

How Can I Write...?

Where Was Humanity?[1]

The walls spoke to me
of the tiptoeing, the whispering,
the all-pervading fear...

Where was then the humanity
in whose ultimate goodness
she so steadfastly held?

Where was humanity at that terrible moment
when she first became aware
of the sound of heavy boots
coming up the stairs?

The truth is that humanity
just... didn't care!

---

1   A visit to Anne Frank's house, June 1985.

At The Museum Of Yad Vashem[1]

At the beginning of the guided tour
she looked so poised and self-assured,
of regal bearing, meticulous dress
with heavy makeup on her face.

I lost sight of her when the tour began –
later, in passing, I saw her again

and was astounded by the change…

her makeup looked worn and disarranged,
her face was crossed by shadows and lines,
an anguished expression dwelt in her eyes.

Later, outside, I saw her again…

her makeup a mess as flanked by friends
she sat on the steps and wept without shame
at the museum of Yad Vashem.

---

1   Israel's Holocaust Martyrs' and Heroes' Remembrance
Authority.

Part Three
Speaking Out

The Poles And The Jews

I am aware that some of the readers of this book may accuse me of harboring "anti-Polish" sentiments. There is no doubt that what I have written here reflects my sense of bitterness at the way the Polish population treated their Jewish fellow-citizens during the Holocaust. The sad fact is that during those years I felt my life being threatened almost as much by my Polish compatriots as by the German occupier.

Having said this, I feel that this point needs further elaboration on my part – if only because I dislike having any "anti…" label attached to my personality. The accusing finger I point now at the Polish people is aimed mainly at the generation of Poles who lived in those years. The sight of an elderly Pole (or, for that matter, of an elderly German, Ukrainian, Lithuanian, Latvian, Croat, etc.) inevitably triggers in my mind the question of where and who he was then. Did he offer help or comfort to his Jewish fellow-citizens? Did he show some compassion and understanding of their plight or did he help hunt them down, did he turn them over to the killers, or even murder them with his own hands?[1]

---

1   Friedlander, Saul "The Years of Extermination", Chapter Eight, p. 536. An entry of Aryeh Klonicki in his diary dated July 7, 1943: … "If it weren't for the hatred of the local inhabitants one could still find a way of hiding. But, as things are it is difficult. Every shepherd or Christian child who sees a Jew immediately reports him to the authorities who lose no time following up these reports. There are some Christians who are ostensibly prepared to hide Jews for full payment. But actually no sooner have they robbed their victims of all their belongings then they hand them over to the authorities. There are some local Christians who have gained distinction in the discovery of Jewish hideouts. There is an eight-year-old boy who loiters all day long in Jewish homes and has uncovered many a hideout."

An honor in the form of the "Righteous Among the Nations" title has been bestowed by Yad Vashem (Israel's Holocaust Martyrs' and Heroes' Remembrance Authority) upon the non-Jewish individuals who risked their lives, freedom and safety in order to rescue Jews from the threat of death without exacting in advance monetary compensation. So far, 6,066 Poles have been honored with this title. Considering the overall size of the Polish population, 35 million at that time, it is clear that such cases were very rare.

Nevertheless, since out of Poland's Jewish pre-war population of 3.5 million some 70,000 survived within Poland's borders, it is likely that many of them owe their lives to some form, direct or indirect, of assistance by ethnic Poles.

On our trip to Poland in the year 2000, it was not difficult to come across signs of a lingering anti-Semitism. There was the swastika smeared on a wall in Krakow (near the site from which the Jews were put on death trains) and the cynical smile on the faces of a couple watching me photographing it. There were the jeers by Polish youth coming from a car which passed us as we mournfully stood at the Umschlagplatz memorial in Warsaw. There was the hostile look which suddenly appeared on the face of the inn-keeper when he realized that we were Jewish. There was the old man, whom we asked for directions in Warsaw, who told us that he knows why the Jews were killed – "it was because they sinned," he stated with unswerving conviction.

In the decades following the Holocaust I have had the opportunity to get to know younger Poles for whom the Holocaust is only history. They seem to be reluctant to speak about their grandparents' generation but what does surface, although very rarely, is an expression of regret at the behavior of Poles in those days. In my correspondence with a Polish lady in Warsaw, she hinted, in one of her letters, to a feeling of "shame" at what had occurred.

Today, for many young, or even middle-aged Poles, the subject of anti-Semitism, and of Jews in general, is probably much less relevant than in the past. This became evident to me during our trip to Poland and was further strengthened by a video film taken by a friend. On his visit to Warsaw with his family he struck up a conversation with a man on the street and in the course of it told him that he is a Jew. The video captured the puzzled expression on the man's face – he didn't seem to see the point. He shrugged and, after a moment's hesitation asked, "So what?" To me, who throughout my years of living in Poland knew that once "identified" by a Pole as a Jew meant being branded for life, this was an eye-opener – it hints at a change toward more tolerance taking place in the minds of many younger Poles.

The vicious anti-Semitism I experienced as a young boy in Europe left me with psychological scars. Even after the Holocaust, and already living in the United States, when making some new acquaintance I would subconsciously ask myself: "Does he know that I am Jewish? How will his attitude towards me change, once he finds out?"

Shortly after arriving in the United States, I began to work. One day one of my fellow-workers, a pleasant guy, asked me casually "What church do you go to?" Forcing myself to overcome a sudden surge of panic I answered "I am Jewish". There, I thought, now he knows…now he will act differently towards me. He did not. To my great surprise about two weeks later he asked me again: "What church do you go to?" I could hardly believe it… I told him that I am Jewish and he has forgotten it…! He has actually forgotten it!!! I am sure that no Pole, no German and no other European would have forgotten my "admission" that I am a Jew. This could happen only in the tolerant, polite society of the great United States.

To those people who, when told of someone's religious preference or racial roots, just shrug their shoulders and ask "So what?", and to those who forget what you told them, I want to say: "May you be many and may you spread your gospel of tolerance throughout the world! The evils of the past cannot be forgotten or forgiven but you are mankind's hope that they will NEVER AGAIN recur in the future!"

Germans? Nazis?

Some years ago I was asked to speak about my Holocaust experiences at our temple in Tel-Aviv. The audience consisted of young people of different nationalities. At the end of my presentation, a young man raised his hand and said: "I am French. My friend here (he pointed to the man sitting near him) is German. He confided in me that he is hurt by the use of the word 'Germans' in Holocaust-related events." He then asked: "Why don't you use the word 'Nazis' instead?" There was no time for a proper reply and, so, I shall now utilize these pages to directly address the Frenchman's German friend.

My dear, young, German fellow:
You will have, undoubtedly, noticed that throughout this book I used the word "Germans" and not "Nazis", as you would have preferred me to do. Why? Because this book is about what I REMEMBER and you may be surprised to learn that throughout the years of the Holocaust I, not even once, heard the word "Nazis"…! I remember hearing only the word "Niemcy" ("Germans" in Polish). I asked other Holocaust survivors, all older than me, and found that they, too, had the same experience. To me, and to them, those coming to murder us were simply "Germans". It was then completely immaterial to us whether they did or did not belong to the NSDAP (Nazi) political party…! When that man burst through our door in the town of Kosów Lacki in 1942, he did not shout "Nazis!" – he screamed that blood-chilling warning "Niemcy!" – a word we came to associate with death and which, for years, struck paralyzing fear into our hearts. It was also immaterial to us whether a particular German was an SS officer, a Wehrmacht soldier or even a civilian – his

being German sufficed to have us see in him someone who has the power to murder us at will. As I am sure you know, the monstrous plan for the "Final Solution Of The Jewish Problem" was set in motion in a suburb of the German capital, and it was the superior German technology which turned the murder of Jews into an industrial-scale genocide. And lest you are tempted to think that a peaceful, innocent majority of the German population had no choice then but to succumb to the terror of Hitler's thugs, let me say this: yes, those thugs were then roaming the streets, beating Jews and looting their stores, but there were also hundreds of ordinary Germans who cheered them on and frequently took part in the action. I know that there were those who tried to stem the Nazi tide. I also know that, beginning with the 1930s, the Nazi hoodlums applied terror tactics to eliminate all opposition. Why did they succeed? Because they had the majority of the people on their side. Most Germans were either supportive of, or sympathetic to, the Nazi ideology. Once the Nazis came to power, there was much popular support for Hitler's regime.

Do you know that, at its peak, the Nazi party numbered 8.2 million members? This translated into roughly one-in-eight Germans – certainly no small minority! I am aware of the arguments that many of those who joined did it for careerist rather than ideological reasons – in order to get better jobs, etc. Yes, joining the Nazi party made life more comfortable for many Germans. And those tens of millions who did not join the party? It was convenient for them to ignore the concentration camps, the Nuremberg Laws, the desecrations of Jewish cemeteries and the pathological filth being spewed out by Nazi newspapers such as "Der Stürmer" and "Der Angriff". And later they also preferred to ask no questions about the hundreds of thousands doing slave-labor in their homes and factories and the tons of human hair and teeth with gold fillings which were pouring into Germany by the train-load from the death camps in occupied East Europe![1]

---

1   Friedlander, Saul "The Years of Extermination", Introduction p. xxii. "...a vast amount of documentary material will show ... that there can be little doubt that by the end of 1942 or early 1943, at the latest,

it became clear to vast numbers of Germans, Poles, Belorussians, Ukrainians and Balts that the Jews were destined for complete extermination."

Ibid., Chapter Five, p. 293. "In the Reich information about the massacres in the East was first and foremost spread by soldiers who often wrote home quite openly about what they witnessed – and quite approvingly as well."

Ibid., Chapter Five, p. 295. "German populations were also quite well informed about the goings-on in the concentration camps, even the most deadly ones."

Ibid., Chapter Six, p. 334. "In other words, as early as during the first months of 1942 even 'ordinary Germans' knew that the Jews were being pitilessly murdered."

One Cannot Comprehend!

One cannot comprehend –
a cattle train with over one hundred people jammed into each of its sixty cars making its way slowly toward Treblinka. Many have already died in the terrible crush. At the camp the gas chambers are working at full capacity and the train gets sidetracked to await its turn. It stands there for hours. Through the walls of the cars and

from the small, barred windows pours out a constant, tearful wail of despair. The annoyed Ukrainian guards yell for the Jews to quiet down. When this doesn't help, they pump shots into the cars. Blood seeps out of the holes in the walls...

The Cattle Car – Up to 100 Jews were crammed into a space of 10 meters (32.8 feet) by 4 meters (13.1 feet) in cattle cars such as these. Some journeys to the death camps lasted for days. Pressed against each other, deprived of water and sanitary facilities, in the intense heat, many died en route or went insane.

One cannot comprehend –
the dreadful moment when the doors of the cattle cars were opened. The shouting, indiscriminate beating, snarling of dogs, the tearing apart of families, the heartrending, last look at dear ones.

One cannot comprehend –
what it's like to be standing naked in the subzero temperature of a Polish winter day waiting to be chased down a narrow lane into a gas chamber.

One cannot comprehend –
the dreadful horror of those fifteen to thirty minutes, after the gas chamber's gate was closed, when in the darkness, carbon monoxide began to stream in, the screams of the victims until the last one ceased to convulse.

One cannot comprehend –
how the German nation allowed itself to be dragged down into the sewers of civilization by a manic, failed-artist, Austrian corporal. Unfortunately, the message in his hate-filled rantings about the "Aryan master race" being destined to rule the world, was music to many German ears. Neither were the Germans unduly perturbed by his explicit calls to violence and to the destruction of the "inferior races", of whom the Jews ranked the lowest.

One cannot comprehend –
how not only common-folk, but also educated, intelligent Germans – professors, clergymen, businessmen, doctors, lawyers… so readily embraced Hitler's delusional, paranoid ideology.[1]

---

1 Friedlander, Saul. "The Years of Extermination", Chapter Ten, p.656. "The major question that challenges all of us is not what personality traits allowed an 'unknown corporal' of the Great War to become the all-powerful leader Adolf Hitler, but rather why tens of millions of Germans blindly followed him to the end, why many still believed in him at the end, and not a few, after the end."

One cannot comprehend –
why so many of those murderers and their accomplices have been allowed to live to this day.

One cannot comprehend –
but the lack of comprehension can in no way obscure the historical facts. This immense monstrous crime has taken place and it was perpetrated by not just a few psychopaths but by tens of thousands who actively murdered and by millions who passively stood by.

Some years ago I happened to watch a TV interview of a German lawyer who, during the war, instead of practicing law practiced murder. Here is what I saw:

A healthy-looking, 80-year-old, former SS-officer, tells his TV interviewer that he did not know what was going on in Treblinka.

"But you were a highly-placed staff officer at the German headquarters in the Warsaw Ghetto and you didn't know?" asks the incredulous interviewer.

"But I was only 28 years old at that time," replies the German.

The interviewer: "You were, in fact, 30 years old then. You are a lawyer by profession, an intelligent person and you were then in your prime, and you are saying that you did not know what was going on in Treblinka? How is this possible?"

The eyes of the old German harden for a moment as he looks at the interviewer. Then his face breaks into a hesitant grin, almost a shy smile, as he slowly shakes his head in modest denial.

"Ah, you overestimate me. I was just a young, insignificant person... I did not know... I had no idea..."

Silence ensues; seconds go by as the two men keep staring at each other, each knowing perfectly well what the other thinks.

The interview ends.

No, one cannot comprehend!

Our "Free-Will" World

In an effort to offer some explanation as to how and why the Holocaust could have happened, theologians, philosophers, spiritual leaders and writers have over the years struggled to find answers. One explanation that is being put forth is that at creation, Man was endowed with "free-will" to run the world as he pleases. According to this concept, if Man's acts result in something that is regarded by humanity as being "Good", he is entitled to reap the rewards. If, on the other hand, his acts result in creating something "Bad", he is to be judged by his fellow-Man and made to face the consequences. Implied in this concept is the absence of divine intervention.

If it is indeed a free-will world we live in, then let us take a look at how good a use Man has made of the generous freedoms this system of values had granted him. Has he built for himself societies which abide by high moral and ethical standards? Has he found ways to live in tolerance, compassion and harmony with his fellow-Man? Is it only the fear of punishment which keeps him from straying into unacceptable, and often, cruel, beast-like behavior? By reviewing mankind's history from the ancient to the modern times – the ceaseless strife, violence, wars, cruelty and wanton bloodshed, one must regretfully conclude that, with few exceptions, Man has largely accumulated a dismal record of abusing the freedoms he has been granted.

I am looking at a photograph[1] showing a group of naked Jews standing in a circle with their backs to the camera, apparently in a pathetic effort to preserve some of their dignity. They are about to be executed by two German machine-gunners. The gunners

---

1   Reprinted from "Jerusalem Post Magazine"; November 22, 1996.

The moments before the slaughter began.

are, obviously, waiting for the order from their officers to start firing. The officers do not appear to be in a hurry – they are seen standing nearby and leisurely talking with one another. On the periphery can be seen at least nine well-clad civilians who came to enjoy the "performance". The two machine-gunners sit idly and relaxed on folding wooden chairs. One of the gunners is seen enjoying a cigarette. On the right of each, on the small tables on which the machine-guns are mounted, can be seen bottles of some beverage with small cups nearby – to quench the thirst of the killers once their "work" is done.

To what level of depravity and moral degradation can Man sink? These killers... these bystanders... these products of the "free-will" system... the very fact that they existed makes mockery of expressions like "Man has been created in divine image" or "Man is the crown of creation" – In this context these words amount to blasphemy!

Let there be no mistake – these killers in the photograph were many then, and there is no reason to believe that others like them do not now walk this earth, ready to commit horrible crimes if given a chance. Apparently, without fear of punishment, Man all too easily metamorphoses into a ruthless killer capable, at whim, of perverting the "free-will" world he has been granted, into a jungle-like world of "kill-at-will". Sadly, we must conclude that the "free-will" system of values, which Man has, presumably, been granted, and Man himself are grossly unsuited for each other.

Crime And Punishment

Implied in the free-will explanation of the Holocaust is the assumption that in the absence of divine intervention it is Man who carries the responsibility to punish his fellow-Man for his transgressions.

I am looking now at a photograph of Kurt Franz,[1] the demonic,

Right: Kurt Franz – nicknamed "Lalka" (doll in Polish) by the prisoners for his good looks – from a mediocre waiter in a Bavarian small-town, second-rate cafe to a cold-blooded, vicious mass killer as commandant of Treblinka.

Left: Supposedly the "administration offices" at Treblinka. (There is an eerie resemblance between this building and the one which housed the "new" gas chambers.

---

1   "The Holocaust Chronicle": Publications International Ltd.; Copyright 2000; pp.475.

sadistic commandant of Treblinka, responsible for the deaths of some 300,000 Jews. It is from a page in his scrapbook entitled "Zeiten", equivalent to something like "The Good Old Times". He stands smiling in his uniform (apparently at some southern resort, judging by the type of trees in the background). Adjacent to this photo is another – of the "administration offices" in Treblinka... After the war Kurt Franz lived in Düsseldorf under his own name and was arrested only in 1959 (!). He was sentenced to life imprisonment, but in 1993 was released "due to old age and health problems". He died in his own home at the age of 81 (!).

Now to another photograph[2] – this one from the album of Karl Hoeker, the adjutant of the commandant of Auschwitz, Richard

SS – men and their female auxiliaries enjoying a day of fun in a resort on the outskirts of Auschwitz – Karl Hoeker in the center.

Baer. Hoeker, who had previously served in the Majdanek camp in Poland, in Auschwitz held the position of administrator of the killing operations and Birkenau. The photograph shows a group of SS-men, including Hoeker and female auxiliaries, standing on

---

2   U.S. Holocaust Memorial Museum; The "Karl Hoeker Album"; Photograph No. 34587.

a wooden bridge and singing cheerfully to the accompaniment of an accordionist. The place: Solaheutte, an Alpine-style recreation lodge on the far reaches of the Auschwitz camp complex, on the banks of the Sola river. This was the place used by the SS to "get away from it all" and enjoy a break from their work of gassing Jews. Hoeker was "tracked down" in Engerhausen, his hometown, only in 1961 (!) where he was working as a bank official. He was found guilty of aiding and abetting the murder of 1,000 Jews on four separate occasions. He served a laughable seven years in prison, and then was released on parole and rehired by his previous employer. He died in the year 2000 at the ripe old age of 88.

So much for the free-will world's commitment to punish the guilty![3]

---

3   It is true that many in the top echelons of the German political and military hierarchy were tried and sentenced to death (as in the Nuremberg trials). However, in the lower rungs, where many were actively involved in the killing process, the punishments meted out were farcical in view of the enormity of the crimes. They are an insult to the memory of the victims!

Where Was He?

The Holocaust challenges Man's faith in humanity and in God.

Recently I came across a Holocaust survivor's story in which the woman helplessly watched from hiding as a Polish policeman coolly took aim and shot her four-year-old sister who was running in terror through an open field. The survivor wrote that at that moment her whole being silently screamed: "Where is God? How can He be so cruel?" In her anguished cry she was asking Him how He can countenance this horror – her question was then being echoed by millions of others.

I clearly recall the words "Gott Mit Uns" (translated: "God Is With Us") on the belt buckles of the German soldiers who roamed the streets of our hometown.

I am now looking at a photograph of a German soldier with his rifle raised, about to execute a Jewish woman holding a

child in her arms.[1] It is likely that those three words were also on the belt buckle of that particular soldier. Was God with him? Absurd, we say! God certainly was not with him and his ilk! But then He, obviously, was also not with that woman and her child about to be murdered! So, WHERE WAS HE? Apparently Man was abandoned, left to run his "free-will" world as he pleased, allowed to run amok in an orgy of death and  destruction, allowed to create hell on earth without fear of divine punishment!

Where was God during the Holocaust? It is likely that to this profound question (just one of many Man asks in his search for God), an answer will never be found. For in order to answer it in a definitive way, Man must first solve the riddle of the creation of the universe which will, likely, forever remain beyond his capabilities.

There is, however, one thing we can state about the Holocaust with absolute certainty – it was a crime planned and perpetrated by Man against his fellow-Man. In the Holocaust, Man's darkest instincts have come to the surface. Man has shown that his mind, which is capable of creating profound works of art, literature and science, can also be used to create engineering drawings for building death camps in which to murder millions of innocent people.[2] Man has shown that his mind can make him into a vicious, evil creature capable of inflicting unspeakable suffering on his fellow-Man.

The question of how the Holocaust could have happened will not be answered by postulating philosophical or theological theories. Any effort to even slightly penetrate the darkness of the

---

1   Reprinted with permission from the Film and Photo Archive, Yad Vashem; Photo No. 143005.

2   As of this writing, Israel's Prime Minister has returned from Germany where he was given the original engineering drawings used in the construction of the Auschwitz-Birkenau death camp where some one million Jews were murdered.

Holocaust should focus on trying to unravel the mystery of the human mind.

Man must never tire of trying to find ways to channel his immense intellect and energy into endeavors which work toward mankind's benefit and not to its detriment. And, most importantly, Man must be made to understand that punishment awaits him if he fails to abide by the basic tenets of humanity's universally accepted codes of moral behavior. Only in this way can mankind ensure that another monstrous crime, such as was the Holocaust, will not recur in the future.

"They Should Have..."

Sometimes I hear a person voice his opinion as to what the Jews of Europe should or should not have done in the years preceding, or during, the Holocaust. In retrospect, we now realize that had the Jewish communities then been better organized, and led by strong, open-minded leaders who had the foresight to correctly assess the approaching danger, many lives might have been saved. However, we need to remind ourselves that in those days the Jews, ever since their exile from their ancestral homeland two thousand years earlier, were a people scattered throughout the world. They were not a homogenous entity led by a central governing body – they lived on sufferance, frequently subjected to the harsh measures of the rulers in the lands in which they lived. Many Jews, particularly those living in Eastern Europe, resided in small villages, known as "shtetls". Their daily lives evolved around eking out a living from small trade and crafts. Their communal activities were invariably, in some way, connected to the religious aspects of their lives. The ritual baths, the burial societies, the charities, the "cheders" where the youngsters learned the Torah, all served to provide them with a common bond and a sense of self-identification. Scholarship was greatly valued and the man who excelled in Torah study was honored and sought after as a good marital match. Not surprisingly, the highest authority in religious, as well as in civil, matters was the local rabbi who was held in great respect and reverence.

No doubt, the Jewish communities of those days were superbly organized to meet the religious and cultural demands of their populations but they were woefully unprepared to meet the challenges which the outside world presented them with on a daily basis. The Jews lived in the midst of hostile populations which proved themselves, on countless occasions to be all too eager, and at the slightest pretext, to stage bloody pogroms. The Jews were ridiculed, humiliated and submitted to all possible indignities, but in most cases their response was "This is God's will; this is our fate". They prayed – the harsher the measures taken against them, the more fervent were their prayers and the stronger their longing for the coming of the Messiah. But their supplications did not help them when the sabers of the Russian Cossacks rained down upon them, or when they were led into the gas chambers built by the Germans.

I harbor no illusions as to the ability of the Jews of those days, being who they were, and living in the world they lived in, to establish effective means of self-defense. Nevertheless, what seemed to be largely missing in their approach to life was an awareness that they ought to try, at least in some measure, to take control of their destinies. There is a saying in Yiddish: "Got helft di vos helfn zich aleyn" which translates into "God helps those who help themselves". I permit myself here to alter this saying into "God helps those who know to defend themselves". Unfortunately, the exclusive reliance on divine protection, and the religious fatalism and passivity of many Jews in those days, proved to be their undoing.

The winds of change began to stir with the birth of modern Zionism in the late nineteenth century and in the period of the Russian Revolution. But this awakening came too late to prepare the Jews to wage an effective self-defense effort during the Holocaust (outstanding exceptions being, of course, the uprisings like the ones in the Warsaw Ghetto and in Treblinka, which, unfortunately, took place only after a large part of the Jewish population had already been murdered).

It is all too easy to criticize the Jews of that time. However, those who were not there will never be able to comprehend the world we lived in – the intense bigotry and humiliating degradation we were exposed to in our daily lives – from being denied the opportunities to work and study to being jeered and beaten on the streets. A Jew's success aroused jealousy and hatred – a Jew's failure was seen as proof of his inferiority and exposed him to ridicule and abuse. Regrettably, organized Christian religion contributed mightily to this social malaise. The incessant hammering of the Christian clergy into the minds of their congregations that the Jews killed their God, served as a constant source of fuel for the flames of hatred.

But why didn't the Jews leave places like Poland when the signs of danger were so clear and real? Why didn't our parents leave when there was still time to do so? They read newspapers, listened to radio, and were not burdened by illusions of divine protection, so why didn't they leave? (My brother reminded me that in 1938, when Germany brutally expelled all Jews of Polish origin from Germany to Poland, one such family whom we personally knew, arrived in Pruszków. Surely they must have given us a first-hand account of what was then going on in Germany – and yet we made no move to leave!). I cannot find it in my heart to point an accusing finger at my parents for the simple reason that I was not "in their shoes". I have no way of knowing the "pros and the cons" they had to weigh while trying to reach a decision. Maybe it was the idea of leaving family behind, or property, friends, or the familiar social surroundings. Maybe it was the hope, the illusion, that the war would not break out, and if it did, somehow all would end on the bright side. Whatever the reasons, they decided to remain in Poland, and we nearly paid with our lives for this decision.

Nevertheless there were some who decided to set all considerations aside and flee. Many of them were single individuals (like Uncle Rywek who fled to Russia), for whom it was easier to take this drastic step. Most, however, were unwilling or unable to leave, and were subsequently caught up in a years-long, nightmarish, life-and-death struggle. Only about two-in-a-hundred survived... we count ourselves very fortunate to be among them.

One must realize that at the time when those fateful decisions by families and individuals had to be made, the human mind was incapable of imagining, even in the remotest way, the possibility that the day might come when human beings would be stuffed into cattle cars and shipped to be asphyxiated in gas chambers.

I have no doubt that had the Jews then known that the German occupation would lead to genocide, most would have made every possible effort to flee (providing, of course, that they had some place to flee to).

So, dear reader, please avoid the temptation to tell us, the survivors, what you think the Jews should or should not have done in those days. You were not there. You can never fully understand what it was like to be there. Also, you can never know how you would have acted had you been faced with the situations the Jew faced, on a daily basis, in those terror-filled years of the Holocaust.

Holocaust "Fatigue"?

As years go by and our numbers inexorably decline, we, the survivors, find ourselves facing the world's changing attitudes toward us. At the very extreme are the Holocaust deniers. These are irrational, absurd individuals for whom facts and history have no meaning. Their very existence makes mockery of man's claim of being an intelligent creature. One could shrug them off as raving lunatics except for the poisonous, dangerous lies they spread.

Then there are those, Jews and non-Jews alike, who grasp the enormity of the Holocaust, its overwhelming impact on the conscience of humanity and on the way Jews now feel and act. They mourn with us and want to learn about the Holocaust by reading, seeing movies and listening to survivors' stories. By doing so, they help perpetuate the memory of the Holocaust.

Then there are other, well-meaning persons, who, after continuous exposure to Holocaust-related events, such as Holocaust Days and survivor stories, develop a certain callousness about it. I find my encounters with these people progressively more painful.

Let there be no mistake, the audiences we face are always attentive and, obviously, highly sympathetic to what we, the survivors, tell them. However, we do begin to detect indications of, what I shall call the "Holocaust Fatigue". At the extreme, these persons tend to completely shy away from Holocaust-related events. After all, they have heard Holocaust survival stories many times already... so yet another one? Yet another letter from a ghetto? Another volume of Holocaust poetry? They probably feel guilty about acting this way, but they argue that the sadness inherent in the Holocaust depresses them. They want to experience joy, hear laughter around them and not listen again and again to the heartbreaking stories from the past. Interestingly, some Holocaust survivors also react this way, although in their case it is because they cannot repeatedly endure reliving the horrors of the past.

At first I thought that it is only I who sensed the creeping inroads this Holocaust "fatigue" is making, but conversations with other survivors revealed that they also share this perception (of course, there is the possibility that we are overly sensitive to the subject and are too easily hurt).

We, Holocaust survivors, also like to have joy and laughter around us and we can understand (up to a certain point) people becoming "fatigued" with what we have to say... and so... many times we just prefer to keep silent... But... it hurts! Yes, it hurts because we know that, like the Passover Haggada, the story of the Holocaust has to be told and retold – it has to be passed on from generation to generation, even at the risk of causing "fatigue"! So listen to us, even though you may have heard us before! Soon we won't be around and all that will remain will be only our written and recorded testimonies. Soon there will remain no one left who will be able to say: "I was there! I saw it!" – no one to answer your questions! Mankind must eternally perpetuate the memory of the Holocaust because forgetting it risks having to experience another one in the future.

Listen To Them Now!

As years go by, the number of Holocaust survivors still alive and able to give oral or written testimony is rapidly decreasing. In another decade or two, the only personal accounts of the Holocaust that will be available, will be those which have been recorded in writing or filmed. As a Holocaust survivor I have had the opportunity to speak on the subject before different audiences. I have often wondered just what impact a personal appearance by a Holocaust survivor has on the audience he addresses.

The difference between reading about Holocaust events and personally hearing about them from a survivor was demonstrated to me quite recently. One Friday evening I read a review of a book dealing with the subject of the 21 notebooks written by Oskar Rosenfeld who, like his counterpart Ringelblum in the Warsaw Ghetto, documented the daily horrors of life in the Lodz Ghetto (Rosenfeld was taken to Auschwitz and murdered there in the fall of 1944).

To quote the book review: "Rosenfeld portrays the horror of the deportations from Lodz, mostly to Chelmno, that began early in 1942… He evinces both the brutal thoroughness of the perpetrators and the inhuman suffering of the Jews…"

The next evening I happened to sit near a man who, I knew, came from Lodz. He is now about 82 years old, wears thick glasses and has a pink-cheeked, young-looking face. I asked him whether he was familiar with that particular book. He turned to me, somewhat startled, and said: "I don't have to read about it… I was there…"

Following is a verbatim account of the conversation which ensued:

I asked him: "How did you survive? Were you in Lodz all the time?"

"I was in the Lodz Ghetto for about two years and then I was deported to Auschwitz."

"When was that?"

"In the fall of 1944."

"With the whole family?"

"With my father and two sisters."

"Where was your mother?"

"She was killed two years earlier, already in 1942."

"How did that happen?"

"She was caught on the street. They just assembled the Jews and held a selection."

"What happened to her?"

"She was sent to Chelmno and killed there."

"How were you taken to Auschwitz? In a train?"

"Yes, in a cattle car but it was only a few hours' ride."

"What happened when you arrived in Auschwitz?"

"When the door of the car opened, there were two Jewish prisoners standing on the platform. Father asked them 'Where are we?' 'In Auschwitz,' one of them said. 'What is here?' Father asked. 'You will soon know,' one of them answered. When we stepped out on the platform, he came closer to me and whispered: 'How old are you?' 'Eighteen,' I replied. 'Tell them that you are nineteen... and take off your glasses; put them in your pocket...'"

"What would have happened had you kept your glasses on?" I asked.

"Mengele sent all those with glasses to the gas chambers."

"What did you do in Auschwitz?"

"All types of work. At times German cattle dealers came looking for laborers and then we had to parade naked, holding our clothes under the left arm, to be checked by a doctor for physical fitness."

"What if one didn't pass the test?"

"He was sent to the gas chambers. After three months I was sent to Dachau where I worked at carrying concrete blocks for building fortifications. At liberation, at the age of 19, I was only one-and-a-half *meters tall and weighed 39 kilograms."*

"Were you together with your family?"

"No, we were immediately separated. My two sisters survived; my father did not."

When I returned home I read again the book review about the Lodz Ghetto. But this time it was different. As I read, I kept seeing that elderly, bespectacled friend of mine – I could hear his voice telling me about events which I was reading about. That man was not talking about "JEWS having been taken to Chelmno" – he was talking about HIS MOTHER having been taken to Chelmno! He was not talking about someone named ROSENFELD having been taken to Auschwitz – he was talking about HIMSELF, HIS FATHER and HIS SISTERS having been taken to Auschwitz!

Yes, the written word is mighty but, when complemented by the spoken word, it is even mightier. So listen to those who were there! In not too long a time their voices will fall silent and you will be left with only lifeless, written words and cold video images.

No doubt on Holocaust Day you will have the opportunity to attend a lecture by a scholarly researcher who will try to analyze the Holocaust from a certain perspective. But will you be listening to a flesh-and-blood survivor tell his story? Will you hear his pained words, look into his eyes and try to understand, at least a fraction, of what he desperately wants you to understand? And the questions you may have – what he remembers, how he survived – are you postponing asking them until it will be too late? (There are so many questions I wish I had asked my parents.) On every visit to the Yad Vashem Holocaust Museum in Jerusalem, I stop at a TV monitor on which a survivor describes the horrors of Treblinka... I ache to ask him a question but... it's always the same words... the same images...

So, listen to them!

Listen to them NOW for soon there will be no one to listen to!

Part Four
Assorted Thoughts And Memories

I Saw Hiroshima, 1945

Some years ago I came across a photograph of Hiroshima as it appeared soon after its devastation by an atomic bomb on August 6, 1945. Strangely, this apocalyptic landscape looked familiar to me... as if I had been there – as if I had once stood among the ruins of Hiroshima... And then, in a flash, I knew...

Early in 1945 we decided to visit recently-liberated Warsaw. It was a bright day as we walked through the "aryan" districts in the general direction of the ghetto. We saw around us a war-ravaged city. There was hardly a street without several damaged buildings. Many had gaping holes in them, obviously caused by artillery shells; in many the roofs and walls showed signs of hits and their windows were shattered. Of some of the buildings only a shell remained – their interiors gutted out by fire. We would walk into them from the street and look up to see beds and sinks hanging precariously above our heads.

The city, despite the bright sunshine, looked drab and depressing. The people who passed us on the street looked apathetic, hollow-eyed and were shabbily dressed. Near many a wall we saw flower wreaths with inscriptions bearing the names of those who were executed there by German firing squads – the stones pockmarked with bullet holes bearing silent evidence of those tragic moments.

I don't recall seeing a trace of the wall which then surrounded the ghetto but at a certain moment we knew without doubt that we had reached our destination. Suddenly, within a few steps, we seemed to have crossed some invisible boundary and found ourselves in a dramatically different, moon-like landscape. In the huge area spread out before us there were no buildings... not any with holes in them, not any with shattered windows, not any

A remaining section of the Warsaw Ghetto wall today.

whole ones and not any burned out ones – there were just, simply, no buildings there!

We climbed a pile of rubble to get a better view of the area. What met our eyes I shall never forget – it was a scene of total destruction! There were no walls over a few feet high left standing. The rubble nearly obliterated the outlines of the streets. It was as if some giant fist had systematically descended upon each and every house and pulverized it, turning the whole area into one big pile of bricks. No buildings… no people… Incredible! Before my eyes flashed memories of four years earlier – streets teeming with humanity, streetcars, peddlers – I heard voices, noises and now… all was still, absolutely still… just the gentle whistling of a morning breeze among the ruins, just the buzzing of flies…

I stood there, a thirteen-year-old, my eyes sweeping the desolate scene. I tried hard to somehow, correlate what I was seeing with what I remembered, but in vain. The scene almost defied credibility.

On That Day In 1945

I saw Hiroshima
before it happened –

I saw it in the ruins
of the Warsaw Ghetto!

The rubble of the Warsaw Ghetto that I saw in 1945.

On The Uss General Sturgis
– From Europe With No Love

As a Jew living in Europe in the years after the Holocaust, I felt myself surrounded by people who were either overtly or covertly hostile to me. Many Poles were hard put to hide their disappointment at seeing that some Jews managed to survive the war. The Germans, though usually behaving correctly towards the survivors, inevitably raised in my mind the question of what they did in the years of the Holocaust. At the Oskar von Miller Polytechnikum in Munich, Germany I was the only Jew in a class of some forty students, all older than I. Judging by their age, most must have been veterans of the German army. They were polite and, on some occasions, even helpful to me. But what did they do THEN?

Members of the faculty were correct and forthcoming but one of the professors made my flesh creep. He was middle-aged with a closely cropped haircut and wrote on the blackboard using the Gothic script. He often cracked jokes and was always rewarded by hearty laughter from the students. I concluded that one had to be a German army veteran to understand his jokes; I had the feeling that he purposely avoided eye contact with me, probably feeling disgusted at seeing a Jew in midst of his Wehrmacht boys.

The people… the proximity to the hundreds of the killing fields scattered throughout Europe, the relentless hostility… all had a deep effect on me. Just how deep this effect was, became clear to me on February 14, 1951, the day on which I with my family (and with hundreds of other war refugees, so called Displaced Persons) left Europe for the United States.

On that day I stood at the stern of the ship USS General Sturgis which was taking us from Bremerhaven, Germany to New York. I was then 18 years old. As the ship was leaving port, I watched the shores of Europe recede into the distance.

I did not know what the future held for me, but I did know what the past was like. Europe mocked and humiliated me from the day of my birth. Europe tried to murder me. Europe robbed me of my childhood – in the years in which I was supposed to attend school and play with my friends, I had to live like a rat in a dungeon under a barn and fear every sound and shadow!

On that day in 1951, on the deck of the General Sturgis, I shed no tears at seeing the shores of Europe disappear from view. The thought which formed in my mind was: "Good riddance! I hope to never again set foot on this mad, blood-soaked continent!"

To this day I am amazed at the change which our relocation to the United States had made in me. With the passage of time, the memories of the old hatreds and persecutions have begun to dim. America has returned to me something which Europe had denied me – the basic human right to live in dignity. That westward voyage on the USS General Sturgis in February 1951 turned out to be a major turning point in my life.

The General Sturgis was no luxury liner. It was built in 1943 and served as a troop carrier in World War Two. On our TransAtlantic crossing, the sea was often choppy and the vessel creaked and groaned (on a subsequent crossing, one month later, it developed a leak and had to be dry-docked for inspection). Every one of the Displaced Persons on board was assigned some task to fulfill in the ship's daily work routine. Since I already had some knowledge of English, I was given the job of an interpreter. No one seemed to mind these "hardships" – we were on our way to the United States and, to us, the ship was already a piece of America.

The crew was friendly and helpful. One day I found myself in the ship's galley in the presence of a few black cooks. One of them laughingly pointed at me and said: "This one is going to be an American sailor!" – prophetic words considering that four years later I was indeed wearing the uniform of a sailor in the United

States Navy.

Just seven months after our arrival, my brother was drafted into the United States Army and shipped back to Germany on... the General Sturgis!

Two years later, upon his discharge from the army he was shipped back to the United States on... again the General Sturgis!

Thus, to us, the name General Sturgis became synonymous with our Exodus from Europe to a new life in the United States.

Tuesday, February 22, 1951: ALL SET FOR A NEW LIFE
The Isadore Koenigstein family is Davenport's newest DP family, arriving here Tuesday. Sponsored by the Jewish community office, the Koenigsteins are residing temporarily with Mr. and Mrs. Abe Greenswag, 1333 West Fourth Street, while searching for a home. Seated are Mr. and Mrs. Koenigstein, and standing are their two sons, Michael, 18, (left) and Jerry, 20. (Times Photo).

Just Waiting For The Question

The following took place in the year 1969 in the city of Saint Louis, Missouri in the United States. The day on which my life was to change dramatically began in a very ordinary manner. I rose at my usual hour and on the way to work I picked up a fellow-worker, a young engineer named Bob. Despite the fact that each one of us knew that the other is Jewish, we never discussed any subject connected with our common religious affiliation.

After exchanging some small talk, we drove on in silence, caught in the usual morning rush hour. Suddenly Bob turned to me and asked: "Would you like to emigrate to Israel?" What happened next does not cease to amaze me to this day. My reply was spontaneous and immediate. Without stopping to weigh any pros and cons, without considering what impact this would have on my life and the life of my family, I said "Yes!" I saw Bob turn quickly toward me and look at me wide-eyed. It was obvious that he did not expect a positive reply, and certainly not within the span of a second. He told me then of a group of representatives from an Israeli company which came into town with the purpose of recruiting engineers. I discussed the matter with my wife (the children were still very young) and a few months later we found ourselves living in Israel.

What happened? What prompted me, a 37-year-old head of a family, a proud citizen of the United States for 20 years to decide on the spur of the moment to leave for a remote little country called Israel? America was good to me. America gave me the opportunity to receive a higher education, to establish a home, to build a career – this was the country which after stifling, hate-filled Europe felt like a breath of fresh air from the moment I set foot on its soil. So what was really behind that spontaneous "Yes" answer to my friend's question?

I close my eyes… images coalesce… memories flash by…

Here I am, a child in the years preceding the outbreak of the Second World War. I see a painting of people praying at a wall and near it a blue-and-white collection box. They hang on a wall in our apartment in Poland. I see a postcard received from a far-off country called Palestine with a tower on its stamp – the tower is called the Tower Of David, "Palestine" is a word I also get to hear on the street. I see a group of Polish youth approaching me. I hear their jeers and shouts of "Jews to Palestine!" I am struck with fear. When one of the boys picks up a stone, I run in the direction of our home. The stone misses me but the message of hatred does not – it embeds itself in my soul to remain and hurt forever.

The darkness of the Holocaust years has descended. I see myself, a ten-year-old boy, hiding for two years under a barn. The people who find shelter with us, frequently speak Yiddish. From them I learn this expressive, universal language of the Jews. I learn Yiddish songs, sung in whispers – those sad and joyous tunes, many conveying the age-old longing of the Jewish people for a homeland in the Land of Israel. Here I hear it said that the Jewish people must have a state, a country of its own, because only then will it be able to defend itself.

The wheels of memory continue turning. I see myself after the war as a youth in a Displaced Persons camp in Germany. I am dancing the "hora" with my friends. Arms on shoulders, legs kicking up in the air – faster and faster we spin and sing with gusto: "Who am I?" and we answer "Israel!" and "Who are you?" and we shout "Israel!" And here I am in a summer camp learning self-defense. We stand in a circle armed with sticks. The instructor barks commands at us… in Hebrew. And here I am standing at a blackboard in a high-school in Munich, Germany. The teacher quizzes me on the subject of geometry… in Hebrew – and I answer him… in Hebrew!

We emigrated from Germany to the United States. Why not to Israel? I did not question my parents' decision. I had complete trust in them.

Our arrival in the United States seemed to put an end to the active phase of my Zionist aspirations. Life began to be normal – university, service in the armed forces, marriage, family, home… The wounds of the past have slowly begun to heal. The memories of the Holocaust began to recede, images to blur.

The Eichmann trial brutally cast us back into the past but, after its conclusion, Time, The Great Healer, began his work again. The Six-Day-War filled us with pride but, essentially, our Zionist activity was limited to buying State of Israel bonds and attending pro-Israel rallies. I realize now that those were the years in which I, subconsciously, tried to delude myself that the words I heard in the dungeon under the barn: "The Jewish people must have a state of its own!" somehow did not apply personally to me. The "Yes" answer which I gave my friend on that day in 1969, was so spontaneous because for years it was waiting to burst forth into the open – because it was an answer which was JUST WAITING FOR THE QUESTION!

Anne, I Understand... [1]

I dedicate these words to the memory of those Jewish children who were murdered when their hiding places were discovered.

The fear... it was still there – even after so many years. Imbedded deeply in every grain of matter, it hung in the air, it radiated from the walls, from the revolving bookcase and from the wooden staircase leading up to her hiding place. The house was crowded with tourists. They milled around casting fleeting glances at the photos and the memorabilia displayed on the walls. Yes, it was there – that all-pervading fear; it enveloped me like a shroud the moment I crossed the threshold, it soaked in through every pore of my body.

I detached myself from the crowd and walked up to an open window. I stood there contemplating the typical Dutch courtyard spread out below me. Most likely it has not changed much since the days when she lived here. How often did she get to see it? Was she, at times, able to steal a glance at the outside world? How often did she stand in this spot wondering what was happening beyond this wall, beyond those trees?

I noticed a photograph of her on one of the walls and stepped up to it. She seemed to be gazing past me, into space. I moved a bit to the side and my eyes met hers. As I looked into them she seemed to come alive. I spoke to her in my thoughts, "Anne, I was almost your age then. I also spent two years in hiding." She seemed to be waiting for me to continue. "I know... I understand what it means to live in constant fear every waking moment, day in and day out, for years. I understand what it means to have to speak in whispers, to tiptoe, to be afraid to cough, to have your heart

1   A visit to Anne Frank's house, June 1985

pound wildly at every unexpected sound or shadow. I understand the depth of your despair when you heard them coming up the stairs, when you realized that all your suffering was in vain, that the end has come. O Anne, I am so sorry about what happened to you!

I turned and walked down the stairs. The wooden steps creaked under my feet – she must have heard them too as she walked down them for the last time. I walked past the bookcase and out of the house.

Only she, that young, dark-haired girl who lived, dreamed and hoped in this house, only she could have understood the emotions which engulfed me then. We both knew the mortal fear, which incessantly gnawed at our young hearts for the duration of two years.

We both lived a life of paralyzing dread, terrorized by the thought that we may be discovered, that we shall hear approaching steps, that we shall be led into the open to be delivered into the hands of merciless killers. Only those who survived in hiding can understand what she felt during those dark years, when the tentacles of a cruel fate kept searching for her… eventually finding, and destroying her.

Anne, I understand… I understand…!

How Could They Have Done It?

W e finished our meal. Wife and daughter left the room and I remained alone at the table with Steve, our son. He was sitting across from me – a nineteen-year old, broad-shouldered with brown hair and blue eyes, on leave from the army. During the meal we did not speak much; our children are not the chatting-type and, therefore, I was not surprised that now, too, Steve was quiet. However, his facial expression told me that something was bothering him, that he wants to speak to me. I was right because he suddenly said: "Dad, I don't understand how they could have done it."

I was stumped. Who is "they" and what have they "done"?

After a few seconds, when he saw that I am not replying, he continued: "They did not live in caves, did not tear raw meat with their hands... so how could they have done such horrible things?"

I understood. Despite the fact that some two weeks have gone by since Holocaust Day, our son has, apparently, not fully recovered from the horrors he saw on television and heard on the radio.

Before I managed to utter a word, he kept on: "Did they not give mankind Bach, Schiller, Beethoven and Goethe? Did they not attend universities, visit museums? Did they not make brilliant contributions to arts and sciences?" He waved his hand for emphasis "so how could they have committed such horrible crimes?"

There is nothing more natural than a son asking questions of his father. When he does, he expects his father to give him a clear answer to what puzzles him. When our son was younger he would ask me questions like "Dad, what is electricity?" and he would receive from me an answer which would reasonably satisfy him. This time, however, the question he threw at me made me feel uneasy.

He sat quietly across from me and waited. I took a deep breath and began "Steve, anti-Semitism is an expression of a deep-rooted, age-old discrimination against Jews in Europe..."

I continued to speak of the pogroms, the first world war, the economic crisis in post-war Germany, Hitler's rise to power and so on. He listened to me in silence but all the time I had the feeling that across from me is sitting a frustrated young man. When I came up for breath, he let go again.

"But, Dad, they read books, attended lectures and concerts, prayed in churches, so how could they...? How could such an intelligent, cultured people murder millions of human beings in cold blood? How could they put them in cattle cars and kill them in gas chambers?"

I tried again, brought up some more historical facts but, increasingly, felt a sense of failure. I was grasping at explanations which did not seem to impress my son. He had heard all this before – he knew all about the high reparations imposed by the Versailles treaty, the massive unemployment, inflation and social unrest which were then plaguing Germany. He wanted to hear something else from me, his father, a Holocaust survivor – he was looking for some reasonable answer to his question and I was not giving it to him. He fell quiet and I thought that our conversation had ended but he was not yet finished with me: "Dad, I just don't understand!" At this moment I realized that all my explanations were a mere camouflage for my real feelings, an act on my part to run away from the truth, from the fact that I am unable to explain something which cannot be explained... The time came to admit defeat – I looked in his eyes and said: "Steve, I also do not understand how they could have done it."

Idek And Marysia[1]

On July 21, in the year 1902, a little boy was born in the city of Pruszków in Poland. He was nicknamed Idek, short for Isadore. On precisely the same day, but nine years later, July 21, 1911, a little girl was born across the street from Idek's home. She was named Mindla but was affectionately called Marysia. The little girl was you, Mother. Unknown to you, the little boy across the street was destined to become the single, most important figure in your life.

The two families had known each other for years. As you grew from infancy to adolescence, Idek began to notice you – in fact, he began to seriously court you when you were only fifteen years old. You were then in high school – a young, carefree girl immersed in your own teenage world and, by your own account, given to much giggling. But you possessed a refreshing, delicate beauty and a warm, vivacious personality which did not escape Idek's attention. Though by then a dashing, and a very eligible, twenty-four-year old bachelor, he became hopelessly enamored in you and asked your parents for your hand once you reach marriageable age. They consented, though in a half-amused manner, thinking it but a youthful infatuation. But they underestimated Idek's determination and the depth of his feelings for you. He set out to conquer your young heart and he went about it in many ways.

Knowing your weakness for sweets, he kept you supplied with candy. Knowing that, in school, drawing was your weak subject, he bought you pencils and crayons, helped you with homework and consoled you when you cried over a low grade. He frequently awaited you at the school gate and walked you home carrying your books. Often, when asked who he was, you were too embarrassed

1   Eulogy for Mother, 1985

to admit that he was your suitor and you replied that he was your older brother. He was tender, thoughtful and unashamedly romantic – openly confessing his love to you and telling others about it.

This heartwarming, touching relationship culminated on February 10th, 1929 – on that day you, Mother, at the age of just seventeen-and-a-half, stood in Pruszków with your Idek under a marriage canopy to become his wife and lifetime companion.

The decade between your marriage and the outbreak of the Second World War were the golden years of your life. You basked in the love of your family and the admiration of your friends. My brother and I came into the world and you showered us with maternal affection. In my earliest memories I see you buttoning my little coat, taking me for walks in a stroller and trying to make me eat by telling me fairy tales.

In Poland, you affectionately called me "Misiu" and in the United States I was "Maytshee" to you until the very last. From you I inherited my love for classical music. To this day I see you sitting at our grand piano and hear the Chopin waltzes you used to play. You had a soft, melodious voice and, as a boy, just a few years old, I used to sing with you. You were a gracious hostess and our home was the frequent site of musical events and discussion groups. You were happy. The future looked solid and secure.

You were only 28 years old when the war broke out. Within the span of just a few days your life, as the lives of countless millions, changed dramatically and irreversibly. You were brutally torn out of your peaceful, comfortable existence and tossed into the fury of the Holocaust. You had to run, hide and live under abominable conditions in constant fear of death. It was a cruel, remorseless, struggle in which your delicate nature often placed you at a disadvantage. But standing at your side was your husband, your Idek, who was ready to sacrifice his life for you. His boundless courage and optimism helped you, and all of us, survive those terrible times.

You were 34 years old when the war ended and in the years which followed, in Europe and in the United States, you worked in offices, stores and factories at your husband's side. But you never really fit into this manner of life. You did not belong on a factory assembly line or behind the cash register of a grocery store – you belonged at home! It was there, in its clean, familiar surroundings that you felt the happiest. You did not seek a career nor strive for riches. After the traumatic years of the war all you wanted was a life of peace and tranquility – to be at home, to take care of your family, to cook, clean, read a book and listen to classical music. But most of the time fate denied you this wish – for nearly forty years you bravely did your share of providing for your family's welfare.

In a world of change and instability there was one unshakable certainty you could always count on – your husband's love and unwavering devotion. You two had your share of disagreements and, at times, tempers flared – but they never diminished the deep affection you felt for each other. I remember my last visit with you, Mother. We were sitting on a sofa and I put my arm around you. You turned to me and said quietly: "This is how your father used to sit with me." You then began to reminisce. You told me how he always kissed you in the morning and when getting up from a meal, and of his other, numerous signs of affection, all of which I remembered so well from my years at home. Then you added wistfully: "I miss my Idek so much!"

In 1978, Father, then a seventy-six-year-old man, came to visit us in Israel for our son's Bar Mitzvah. You were unable to travel and so he came alone. A few days after his arrival I went out with him for an evening stroll. He confessed to me that he missed you very much. I remember to this day what he said: "I love her today as much as I did on the day when she became my bride. I shall never again travel anywhere without my beloved Marysia." And he did not – since then he has not left your side until the end of his life. You were 69 years old when he passed away and his death was a blow from which you never recovered.

Mother, on February 10th, 1929, you stood with your beloved Idek under a marriage canopy. On February 10th, 1985, on your 56th wedding anniversary, you were buried at his side...

He was waiting for you,
under a canopy eternal and vast,

and, as you were lowered into the earth,
he lifted you into his arms
and, as of old, kissed your face,
your lips, your eyes,

and whispered to you,
"It is I... it is I... – your Idek."

You came to me today,
as you did so long ago,
to lie at my side...

I shall never again
travel without you,
my dear Marysiu,
my eternal bride...

Thanks, Dad![1]

Steve, you are playing an important role at this Sabbath morning service. As the Bar Mitzvah boy, you are at the center of this joyous occasion and the attention of those assembled here is, naturally, focused upon you. However, without in any way diminishing the importance of your part in today's festivities, I wish, with your permission, to address some remarks to another person present with us in this room. I want to use this opportunity to honor a man but for whose gift to me we would not be now celebrating your Bar Mitzvah. The man I am referring to is my father, Isadore, who came from the United States for this occasion and is here with us now. The gift he gave me is the most precious of all – the gift of life. However, he did not give it to me only once, through the normal process of parenthood, but again and again, for countless times, when for six long years he fought to protect our family from a cruel fate for which we seemed to be destined. Those were the years of the Holocaust when six million Jews were murdered in Europe – systematically, in cold blood, shot in the streets, hunted down in forests, asphyxiated in gas chambers. Those were the years when Jewish lives could be taken with impunity – by anyone, at any time – when every Jew still alive was the equivalent of a miracle – a candle continuing to burn in the midst of a howling storm, its flame flickering in the darkness, fighting desperately against overwhelming odds.

I was seven years old when the war broke out and thirteen, your age now, Stevie, when it ended. I was young, only a child, but the horror of those days in Poland remains deeply engraved

1   Excerpt from my presentation delivered on September 9, 1978 at our son Steve's Bar Mitzvah at the Ramat Aviv congregation in Tel Aviv.

on my mind. I hear doors open, people shouting, running, hiding, crawling into holes and basements, fleeing into fields and forests, the panic, the shots... I remember the times when fear gripped me in a steel vise, when my heart beat like a hammer and my whole being cried in anguish: "No, please, let not this be the end, please, please!" – a young boy facing the paralyzing realization that within moments all may cease... overcome by self-pity, bitter tears welling up in his eyes, angry – at everything, at everybody, asking "Why? Why now? Why must it all end now?"

Dad, in the years following the war we did not speak often of the Holocaust. It was all so painful and the memories were still so fresh. After liberation we went to see Treblinka but in the five years of living in Munich we never once visited Dachau, a scant twenty kilometers away. We wanted to forget, to start a new life. Our nerves were taut; for a long time the sound of a slamming door, or a sudden shout would tighten my insides into a knot. Gradually, life became peaceful, filled with work, school and normal everyday concerns. We preferred to look towards the future instead of dwelling in the past. We did not let the past turn us into cynics nor blind us to the beauties of the world. We enjoy the pleasures of life and appreciate human love and kindness. But the wounds are there, only partly healed and easily reopened. To this day I find myself lacking courage to open a book or see a movie dealing with the Holocaust. I was looking for an excuse not to watch the "Holocaust" television series until, literally, seconds before it came on the air. News of the revival of Nazism, of mock trials and acquittals of mass murderers or outright denials of the Holocaust – all grate on raw nerves and reopen the wounds.

The mournful sound of sirens on Holocaust Day... traffic halting... people stepping out of their cars, standing with heads bowed. The grandmotherly-looking woman sitting near me on the bus; I notice the concentration camp number on her arm... what tales of anguish and suffering could she recount? The elderly man who tells me that his present family is his "second" one; he had a family before the war – wife, children, parents, brothers, sisters... all gone! Whole Jewish populations... vanished, wiped out! Yes, the wounds are there and will never heal.

At times, when confronted too vividly with the past, I am overcome by bitterness and anger. How was such a thing allowed to happen? Why was this slaughter permitted to go on year after year until only about two-out-of-a-hundred remained alive? Why have the murderers not all been punished? I am not the only one asking these questions – they are being asked by millions throughout the world. Humanity asks, debates, and philosophizes over them – some even claim to have found answers. But what answer will satisfy the man whose family was murdered? Will philosophical arguments satisfy him? Maybe there is no answer. Or maybe, intuitively, Man knows what the answer is but is unwilling to admit it, lest it destroy his self-esteem and make mockery of the cherished beliefs he has of himself.

Dad, as I get older I find myself viewing the Holocaust from a changing perspective. The enormity of it all overwhelms me. I realize that I am now roughly the same age you were then and that our children are now, approximately, as old as my brother and I were in those days. I now appreciate and better understand the agonies you and Mother must have suffered in your struggle to save us. I sometimes wonder whether I would be able to do for our children what you did for yours.

Dad, from the earliest days of my childhood I remember you as a cheerful individual, always brimming with energy and a perpetual optimist. You were, and still are, an excitable person and rather stubborn at times. You never cease planning, hoping, dreaming and the energy pent up in you is forever seeking an outlet. All of these characteristics served you, and us, in good stead during the war. You never gave up. You never let your inner doubts and torments come to the surface and affect others. Your optimism sustained us during the darkest hours and gave us hope that we shall survive. We clung to your words because they were the words we wanted to hear. Even at the depths of our ordeal you would not let despair overtake us. You just, simply, would not give up. Always the fighter, always saying that we shall survive – and you were right – we did.

Thanks to you our home has always been a Zionist one. You carry in your heart a great love for the State of Israel. I remember the surge of emotions on your face when, several years ago, in the cool air of a Jerusalem evening, you looked for the first time at the ancient stones of the Western Wall – you touched them... there were tears in your eyes... You insisted that you must see Masada. I took you there. You spent hours in the heat of an August afternoon exploring the heroic past of our people.

Dad, for many years I have been vaguely aware of a feeling that there is something I want to tell you, something I ought to say to you. But as years were going by, this feeling remained undefined and unsaid. It was only a few days ago, when I looked at you – here in Israel – for the Bar Mitzvah of your grandson, that I suddenly understood... What I want to say to you today is simply "Thanks, dad...". Thanks for accomplishing the nearly impossible – the chances of a Jewish family of four surviving the Holocaust together were almost nil. But you did it by fighting stubbornly against all odds, by, virtually, bending the course of fate through the sheer force of your will.

Steve, remember what was said here today. Hold your head high and don't ever hesitate to stand up for your rights and for the rights of our people to live in dignity and peace. Be constantly on your guard against prejudice and hatred. Let the past teach but not sadden you. Enjoy life and the beauty of the world around you. Give love and you will receive love in return. Be polite, kind and just in all you do. Be a good citizen of your country and of the world. Get to know your roots – learn our culture, heritage and history. Learn why the State of Israel came into being – so that Jews will never again have to run and hide in basements, attics and barns – so that there will be no more ghettos and concentration camps, no more wanton spilling of Jewish blood – so that neither you, nor any Jewish parents for generations to come, will have to suffer the ordeal of having to save their children from a holocaust. May God bless you, my son.

The Hat[1]

A year has passed since you left us, Father, but I still see you everywhere. The house is still so full of your presence. I see you sitting behind the kitchen table absorbed in reading the newspaper. I hear you in the morning getting dressed, speaking in low tones to Mother. You smile at me from the picture above my bed.

I open the drawer and see your glasses – they look so forlorn, waiting in vain to be placed on your nose. I open the closet and see your shirts hanging limply, never again to be filled with your small corpulent body. Your shoes look so sad and lonely – they seem to know that they are never again to feel the warmth of your feet.

My eyes fall upon your hat lying on a shelf. I pick it up and gently hold it in my hands. My fingers slowly trace out its contours and probe the empty space within it. I stand still, lost in thought.

Suddenly my mind races back forty years to the town of Kosów Lacki in wartime Poland. I see another hat – a large gray one. It is hanging on a peg above the bed upon which you, Father, and I are lying fully dressed. We have just returned from the funeral of your father, my grandfather Hanoch. You are holding your arm tight around me. Tears are rolling down your face. Your eyes wander up to the hat. I hear you sigh deeply and whisper in a choked voice: "here is the hat… here is the hat… but where is the dear head it covered?"

Forty years later, as I stand holding your hat in my hands, I hear those words again, and I know that life has completed another one of its eternal cycles – it is now my turn to say what you said then.

---

1   Written in 1981

From deep within my soul a cry begins to mount, a lament to rise, a mournful tone begins to intone:

Here is your hat... here is your hat...
my Father,
but where is the dear head it covered?

Where is that gentle face
which always befriended, becharmed?
Where are the kisses you always bestowed,
where is the squeeze of your arms?

Where are those gentle, brown eyes of yours
which always sparkled with cheer and wit?
Closed were your eyelids the last time I saw them –
as cold as ice to the touch of my lips...

Wherever I look, I see your face;
I miss you so much, oh, Father!

Here is the hat... here is the hat...
but where is the head,
it covered?

Oren Lubinski's Bar Mitzvah[1]

Dear Oren:

Your Bar Mitzvah, an event so significant in your life, is an emotional experience for all of us. For me, this day is especially moving and memory-evoking. This, without doubt, is due to the way the subject of "Bar Mitzvah" relates to the events I experienced in childhood.

I was born in Poland to a well-to-do, loving family. My parents had a comfortable and secure future planned for me. I was to receive a higher education, a career and, almost certainly, the day would come when I would stand in front of a congregation somewhere in Poland and speak, likely in Polish, at the Bar Mitzvah of a grandson.

However, the chances of all this becoming reality began to fade almost from the day of my birth. I was an infant three months old when the Nazis came to power in Germany. The Second World War broke out one month before my seventh birthday. I was a nine-year-old boy when the leaders of the German Reich assembled in a Berlin suburb called Wannsee and decided to murder every Jewish man, woman and child wherever they may be. The civilian and military leaders of a big, modern country with a powerful army, a huge industrial base and advanced technology, decided to exterminate a defenseless, civilian population in its entirety, because it considered it racially inferior. There, in Wannsee, on the twentieth of January, 1942, a death sentence was pronounced on me, on my family, and on the entire Jewish people.

Oren, we tend to think of the Bar Mitzvah ritual as something that is obvious and assured to every Jewish youngster. Every Jewish

---

1   Delivered in Hebrew on November 1, 2003 at our grandson's, Oren's, Bar Mitzvah at the Beit Daniel congregation in Tel Aviv.

boy knows that, upon reaching the age of thirteen, he will be Bar Mitzvah. And this is his right – this is the way it should be! It is the duty of his family, and of the community he lives in, to provide him with all the means necessary to take advantage of this right. Unfortunately, this is not what always happens – among the six million victims of the Holocaust were one-and-a-half million children, many of them under Bar Mitzvah age. Their right to experience what you, Oren, experienced here this morning, was denied to them for eternity. They were murdered and the synagogues in which they were to become Bney-Mitzvah were destroyed. In another ten days we shall be commemorating the sixty-fifth anniversary of "Kristallnacht" – an event in which the Nazis, in one night, burned 267 synagogues throughout Germany and Austria. In Eastern Europe under German occupation, thousands of synagogues were burned, some with Jewish men, women and children crammed into them.

The first Bar Mitzvah I attended took place in the year 1939 in Warsaw, the capital of Poland. The city was besieged by the Germans and was being mercilessly pounded by artillery and from the air. The little, dark room in which the Bar Mitzvah took place remains engraved in my memory. It was packed with people standing shoulder-to-shoulder. There was no ventilation and the room was stifling hot. Light was provided by few candles placed near the Torah scrolls. The Bar Mitzvah boy had difficulty seeing the text – at a certain point he stopped reading and broke down in tears. Many in the crowd began crying with him. That Bar Mitzvah left me, then a seven-year-old boy, with heavy, sad memories.

My brother, Jerry, reached Bar Mitzvah age in the year 1943, the most horrible year of the Holocaust. The gas chambers at the death camp Treblinka were then killing 18,000 Jews a day! We were in hiding, just a short distance from that inferno. The only concern that, then, occupied our minds was how to survive yet another day. Birthdays…? Bar Mitzvahs…? They belonged to another, an almost abstract, world – a world in which we sat on chairs, slept in beds and walked on streets…There, in the damp, dark dungeon under a barn, engulfed by a pervasive, perpetual fear, the subject of birthdays was never even mentioned. My brother's right to be Bar Mitzvah was denied to him!

I reached Bar Mitzvah age in the year 1945 after our return to our hometown, Pruszków. We returned to a town empty of Jews. Out of the three-thousand Jews who lived there before the war, only thirty, that is, only one-out-of-a-hundred survived. No trace of Jewish life and its communal institutions remained – the whole Jewish population vanished as if it never existed – no rabbi… no cantor…no synagogue! My thirteenth birthday came and went. I, too, was denied my right to be Bar Mitzvah!

Oren, try to grasp the significance and the symbolism of the event which took place here just a while ago. This morning there were placed at your disposal a beautiful, modern synagogue, a rabbi, a cantor, a loving family and this honorable congregation of guests. This morning you were able to take advantage of your right to be Bar Mitzvah (and you have done it in a most dignified manner). By reading from the Torah you have honored the memory of those million-and-a-half young victims of the Holocaust.

Try to understand what it means for me to be present at this event – for me, who barely managed to escape the fate of those murdered children!

Oren, your Bar Mitzvah deeply moves me because it is not taking place in a foreign land but in our homeland, Israel. It moves me because I am delivering these words in Hebrew, our national language. It moves me because I see in you a link in the eternal chain of the Jewish people which our enemies have not been, and never will be, able to break. I am moved because the forces of evil which prevented me and my brother from being Bar Mitzvah, have not been able to do this to you.

Oren, this is a day of joy for you and for all of us. My words relating to the events in the past were not meant to make you sad, but only aware of what had happened. We must learn from the past, for he who does not do so, may be faced with similar ordeals in the future. The Noah portion of the Torah, which was read this morning, tells us that alongside the Good in man, also resides Evil. There is much evil in this world. It behooves us to be aware of it and, if necessary, to fight it.

Generations come and generations go. In a number of years your generation, Oren, will replace ours. You will be the ones who will lead our nation. You will be the ones who will determine our moral and cultural standards. Therefore, it is so important that your generation should mature within a proper framework of values: of respect for fellow-man, of high moral standards and personal integrity, of respect for property – yours, as well as of others, and of respect and protection of nature and the animal world.

Oren, contribute your part in strengthening the Good which is in Man. Do your share in trying to improve the world we live in. Be proud of being a Jew and a citizen of the State of Israel! Learn the history and the heritage of our people and do not let what you learned fade from your memory – keep it alive! Tell it to your children so they may tell it to theirs… this way you will do your share in assuring that the Jewish people and Israel will live forever!

Accept my, Nomi's, and the whole family's loving wishes for a happy and successful future!

This Has To Be Said[1]

We walked out of the building into the open. I remained behind the others in the group; in situations in which I come face-to-face with the history of the Holocaust, I prefer to be alone. I find myself becoming easily irritated and not tolerant of idle conversations.

The photographs had their predictable impact on me. I felt sad and angry – sad after having once again looked into the eyes of those about to die of starvation, of those peering out of slits in the cattle cars which will take them to their deaths, of those standing naked at the edges of execution pits. I felt angry at humanity, at the world, at everyone and everything for letting such horrible crimes take place.

And once again I was overwhelmed by a feeling of gratitude toward my parents, and to whoever or whatever allowed me to escape the terrible fate which awaited me. I had been there. How easily I could have been that emaciated child sitting on the sidewalk in the Warsaw Ghetto! How easily I could have been that child being marched to a death transport surrounded by helmeted, gun-toting German soldiers! My name could easily have been among those being called out in the darkness of the pavilion erected in memory of the million and a half murdered Jewish children.

I walked out into the open, glad to leave behind the milling crowd of tourists. Whenever I see tourists at Holocaust memorial sites I cannot help being torn by conflicting emotions. On one hand I am glad that people from all over the world come to see what bigotry and blind hatred can lead to. On the other hand,

---

1   Overheard at Yad Vashem, Israel Holocaust Museum; July, 2000.

I cannot shake the feeling that, for the tourist, this may be just another site on his sightseeing itinerary, just another item to be crossed off the list at the end of a touring day.

I wonder – did they learn anything? Did the things they saw stir their conscience, change their world outlook? Will they be willing, or able, to pass their feelings on to others?

As I walked out of the museum I became aware of the scent of pine trees. I like this aroma, but, to this day, it causes unpleasant flashbacks. It is so typical of the smell of Polish forests. After we were liberated, we rode in a horse-drawn buggy to see Treblinka, and there were pine trees along the way.

It was an unusually hot day in Jerusalem and people walked slowly. Many took shelter underneath the trees lining the Alley Of the Righteous Gentiles. As I walked, I noticed a man, a woman and a child sitting under one of the trees. As I drew closer I realized they were speaking German. There was nothing unusual about this; many German tourists visit Yad Vashem every year. The man had a short beard and looked to be in his thirties. His young wife sat on the bench near him and their daughter, a few years old, sat on the ground at her father's feet. The man was speaking and I could overhear a few words. Eavesdropping is not polite, but something I heard made me slow down.

The man was saying, "Man sagt der ist schuldig... der ist schuldig" ("People say this one is guilty...that one is guilty".) There was a pause and then he said, raising his voice, "Aber das war doch Deutschland!" ("But this was Germany!"). He then repeated, with emphasis, "Aber das war doch Deutschland!"

I stood riveted to the spot, pretending to be studying a map. For a while no one said anything. I cast a glance in the direction of the family and saw the woman and child looking intently at the man. He spoke again, forcefully, "Das muss man doch aussprechen!" ("This has to be said!") and then again, in an almost angry tone, "Das muss man doch aussprechen!"

Silence ensued. As I began to slowly walk away, I heard the woman speak. She was asking a question and I caught only the last two words, "...sechs millionen??" ("Six million?") The man's reply, uttered in a subdued, dejected tone, reached me clearly, "Ja, sechs millionen." ("Yes, six million").

I continued slowly in the sun-drenched square of Yad Vashem, struck by the significance of what I just heard. I had just overheard a young German father make his family face the ugly truth about his nation's past. Here in Jerusalem, in the Alley Of The Righteous Gentiles in Yad Vashem, I heard one young German family trying to come to grips with the past and learn from it.

If there are more like them, then maybe the world of tomorrow will be a better place to live in.

OPINION   The Jerusalem Post   Friday, April 3, 1992   7A

Science is again being perverted

Michael Koenig

RECENTLY, I came across a report in the Hebrew press in which Walter Luftel, president of the Austrian Engineers and Architects Association, is said to have announced, after having conducted a professional study, that the Holocaust could not have happened. He conducted this study at the request of a German lawyer and is said to have submitted his conclusions to the Viennese newspaper *Die Presse*. He claims that the gas Zyklon B could not have killed so many people and that the cremation of such huge numbers of bodies would have been impossible.

Mr. Luftel bases his professional verdict on "laws of nature" – the human body, he states, is basically not combustible and enormous amounts of energy, time and organizational effort would be needed to cremate so many people. He further substantiates his "judgment" by stating that the crematoria were not big enough to have handled the claimed number of Holocaust victims.

I was shocked by the news report. I had, of course, heard of "Holocaust deniers," but always thought them a small group of uneducated crackpots. However, this "engineering study" was done by no less than the president of the Engineers and Architects Association of Austria – undoubtedly a very educated man and a prominent figure in Austrian society. As a human being, a Holocaust sur-

ing and abhorrent.

Mr. Luftel is right – the human body is, basically, not combustible. This is the reason why the Kommandant of Treblinka failed in his early attempts to burn the exhumed bodies of the camp's 750,000 victims. The corpses would not burn no matter how much gasoline was poured into the pits. He was forced to call for help which arrived in the person of a

four crematoria, with a combined capacity of 4,456 corpses a day, were in use from March 22 until June 28, 1943. But even at this, vastly improved, facility there were times when the crematoria could not cope with the output of the gas chambers – they occasionally broke down and so corpses were also buried in pits.

As relates to the killing capacity of Zyklon B: It is amazing what a few

'Professional' engineering studies were used then to help kill six million, and now to deny the existence of the Holocaust

certain Herbert Floss who, too, did a "professional" study of this matter. He did thorough time-study work to determine how many bodies can be exhumed and carried per hour and performed trial burnings on samples of the "raw material" – this way he found that the old bodies burned better than the new ones and the fat ones better than the thin ones. Ingeniously, he erected huge pyres on cement pillars, overlaid them with rails and reached the processing rate of 10,000 bodies a day – a remarkable engineering achievement, indeed.

I don't know how old Mr. Luftel is and where he was in those days, but I can tell him where I was then. I was hiding for two years in a small dungeon under a barn just a short distance from Treblinka. I saw the huge columns of smoke rising into the sky and breathed the awful stench of

canisters of this stuff can do when thrown into a hermetically sealed chamber jammed with hundreds of compressed naked human bodies. But, in a way, Mr. Luftel is right in questioning Zyklon B's capabilities. It took the victims anywhere from 20 minutes to half an hour to die – what a waste of valuable time! Just imagine, Mr. Luftel, what a more efficient gas could have accomplished – one that would kill in, say, five minutes – what a tremendous jump in productivity could have been realized!

Would Mr. Luftel like to see a photograph I have of an invoice sent by the Degesch Co. of Frankfurt to Herr Obersturmführer Kurt Gerstein in Berlin? It is just one of numerous such documents attesting to the nature of German engineering activity in the 1940s.

Countless books have been writ-

ten, museums and memorials erected, testimonies of thousands (including those of the Nazi perpetrators) recorded – but Mr. Luftel's professional study concludes that the Holocaust never took place! Would a visit to Auschwitz, Treblinka, Sobibor, Majdanek and other such monuments to German engineering induce him to change his mind?

Perhaps Mr. Luftel could help me answer a question which has puzzled me for a long time. If the Holocaust never took place, where did those six million European Jews disappear to? Are they, and their descendants, hiding somewhere all these years, part of a sinister worldwide Jewish conspiracy to discredit the Austrian and the German people? Where did the complete Jewish population of my hometown in Poland disappear to?

Why are people like Mr. Luftel and his German lawyer-friend making such efforts now to deny the Holocaust? Would it not be simpler to wait another decade or two when all those Jews with tattooed arms, and all those with the stench of burning bodies in their nostrils, will be gone?

Should Mr. Luftel have been misquoted, then I shall readily extend to him my apologies for the harsh words I have written here. But if the statements attributed to him have been made, then I ask him to refute and repudiate them. This would help erase the ugly stain which his ignominious attempt to falsify history by using technical arguments has placed on the engineering profession.

The writer resides in Ramat Aviv.

Some Thoughts

The Holocaust has left many of us, the survivors, with traumatic memories of just how thin was the line on which our lives were then hanging. These memories continue, in varying degrees, to affect our outlook on life. For some survivors, the burden of their memories proved unbearable and led them to confinement in mental institutions. Most survivors, though, managed to return to regular lives. They became productive, and often leading, members of the societies they live in.

The depth of an individual survivor's trauma depends, in great measure, on the circumstances under which he survived and undoubtedly, on his age at that time. The scars tend to be deeper the greater was the personal exposure to the horrors of those years and the older the person was at that time. I was fortunate in many ways. During the peak years of the Holocaust (1941 to 1944) I was a youngster only nine-to-twelve years old. I survived in, what might be considered, "privileged" circumstances. I had my parents with me and it was on their shoulders, not mine, where the burden of ensuring our survival rested. I survived in hiding thus escaping the horrors of concentration camps. Yes, indeed, I was fortunate and yet... those years remain indelibly etched in my memory as years of horror, as years of a deep, personal trauma. One should not be tempted to try to compare the suffering of one Holocaust survivor to the suffering of another. Every single one of us, regardless of how we survived – whether under an assumed identity, in hiding, in forests or in concentration camps, has his own, anguished story to tell. However, there is one thing in common to all of our stories: the all-pervasive, debilitating, paralyzing fear which haunted us for every moment of every day for the duration of years.

Today at the age of seventy-nine, as I review my past, I can discern three major, Holocaust-related, events which profoundly affected the course of my life. In chronological order, the first occurred on the day of liberation in 1944 when I stepped out from the barn into the open. On that day my right to stay alive was returned to me.

The second event, in 1951, was my voyage from Europe to America on the USS General Sturgis – my arrival in the United States restored to me the right to which every human being is entitled (and which Europe has denied me) – the right to live my life in freedom and dignity.

The third event was my arrival in Israel in 1970. I took this step because the Holocaust has robbed me of any illusion that if my life is again threatened for the single reason that I am a Jew, the nations of the world will come to my rescue. As the Holocaust was raging and its details were already well known, the nations of the world could not spare even a single bomb to be dropped on the railroad tracks leading to Auschwitz-Birkenau (while conducting regular reconnaissance flights over the death camp and heavy bombing raids on factory areas less than five miles from the gas chambers).[1] I have read all the arguments and explanations of why this was not done and they sound hollow to me. Disruptions in the schedule of the trains bringing victims to the gas chambers of Auschwitz-Birkenau could have saved lives! But these were JEWISH lives and they were then, and may also be in the future, considered expendable.

NOT MINE!

NEVER AGAIN!

---

1   "The Holocaust Chronicle" Publications International Ltd., p. 554.

CPSIA information can be obtained
at www.ICGtesting.com
Printed in the USA
FFOW01n0709290415
13028FF